Why do I do t

For Bill and Elizabeth,
who gave me the freedom to find my own way

Why do I do this every day?

Finding meaning in your work

Fraser Dyer

A LION BOOK

A Lion Book
an imprint of
Lion Hudson plc
Mayfield House, 256 Banbury Road,
Oxford OX2 7DH, England
www.lionhudson.com
ISBN 0 7459 5171 6

First edition 2005
10 9 8 7 6 5 4 3 2 1 0

A catalogue record for this book is available
from the British Library

Typeset in 10/13 Latin725 BT

Printed and bound in Great Britain
by Cox & Wyman Ltd, Reading

Contents

Introduction

If you are in full-time work, then you probably spend at least eight hours a day doing your job. That makes it the single biggest activity you engage in apart from sleep so it therefore seems logical that you will want to spend this time doing something that is rewarding, fulfilling and meaningful.

Yet for many people that is not the reality of their working life, and not just those who are in supposedly 'boring' jobs. An increasing number of people who have a career are expressing frustration and disappointment with the way it has turned out.

I first became aware of this trend over a decade ago when I was in my late twenties. As people my age were approaching their thirtieth birthdays, a kind of disenchantment began to seep into their conversation. And when I set up my management coaching business, it became clear just how prevalent this phenomenon is. As clients began to work through the challenges they faced in their jobs, it emerged that many of them weren't terribly motivated to implement the solutions we'd discussed. When challenged about their lack of action, the truth came out. 'Actually, the heart of the problem is that I've had enough of this job; but I just can't figure out what I'd like to do instead.' Some would also say, 'I'd even be willing to go back to university if only I could find my niche.'

Many of today's generation of thirty- and forty-somethings have discovered that there is a significant gap between the expectations about work that they grew up with and the reality they have encountered. And this has left them questioning where their career is heading and whether there isn't a more fulfilling or purposeful working life out there waiting for them to discover.

How did this come about? Why do so many people feel that their work lacks any meaning? And what right have they got to expect work to be fun anyway? Every other generation has knuckled down and done their duty. Why can't they just stiffen the old upper lip and get on with it?

Today's generation of workers were pre-programmed to work hard at school to get into the university course of their choice, which in turn would lead to a solid career for life and let them retire on a fat pension. It worked for the baby-boom generation so they had good grounds to expect the same for themselves. In fact, many of my peers were the first generation in their family to go to university. They had opportunities their parents never had. They felt lucky and privileged and, quite reasonably, expected their education to deliver a better quality of working life than mum and dad had ever had. Finding themselves gradually disillusioned was not only a let-down but for many a source of guilt.

As my coaching business took a new direction, I began helping clients to unpack the reasons for their disillusionment, encouraging them to find new ways to think about their career that would enable them to become clearer about what they wanted to do with their lives.

The core of this work has been enabling people to regain a sense of vocation. The very word vocation has always been associated with a particular group of professions – teaching, medicine, ministry and so on. Yet I don't believe that a vocational working life is the reserve of these few. It is available to all.

When I use the word 'vocation', I am describing a working life that involves more than just a job. It is work that somehow connects to the individual on a deeper level and which taps into their sense of purpose, spirit and meaning. A vocation involves work that is congruent with your personal values, makes best use of your talents and abilities and allows you to fulfil your potential. It also has an impact on others in some way; the vocational worker has a sense that their labour really makes a difference. This feeling that one's work has some significant *meaning* is, I believe, at the heart of many people's quest for a better experience of work.

In *Why Do I Do This Every Day?*, I outline some of the factors that have contributed to the disaffection that workers feel for their careers. The first chapter may seem a somewhat gloomy catalogue of the changing nature of work and of the occupational trends that are getting people down. Yet many of the changes we have seen in the culture of work over the last two decades have also created exciting new opportunities that enable those who are willing to bite the bullet to claim a vocational working life. And so I also look at how today's workers can capitalize on the opportunities that are presented by changes in the workplace.

The bulk of the book looks at different components of meaningful work and is designed to help the reader better understand and articulate what they are looking for in their career. They can then spot the opportunities (or create them) that resonate with their sense of vocation.

While I use the word 'vocation' to describe work that is a tangible expression of who you are, I see the idea of a career somewhat differently. First, I believe a person's vocation can be expressed in more than one way, so it is possible for a worker to pursue their vocation in more than one job or career. But, secondly, I see the defining quality of a career as being a job that offers some route for advancement or progression within a particular line of work. So a person may have several jobs as part of a career in, say, accountancy, where they develop and are promoted within that profession. Perhaps they move to different companies in the process but nonetheless they can trace the continuity in their line of work.

When someone considers a career change, they are really looking at a radical shift in their work – jumping track, as it were. A person seeking to fulfil their vocation might consider such a change but equally a person who is already fulfilling their vocation in one field of work could potentially consider the next phase of their vocation in a different career.

In this model of work, the thread of continuity is the worker's sense of vocation, where they hold true to their values and deeper quest for purpose and meaning in their work. Given that the opportunities for having a 'career for life' have been eroded by the changing culture of work, I believe the new survival strategy for workers is to gain clarity about their vocation and use that as a guiding light for the career choices they make. This is a departure from conventional thinking about careers, which saw the established and assumed routes of progression in a profession as the way to pursue professional advancement.

The book rests on an assumption that it is the work we do that adds meaning and fulfilment to our lives. That needn't, incidentally, be paid work. Some people's vocation finds expression through voluntary work or an unwaged domestic or family role. I'm aware that this isn't a view shared by all, and I know that some psychologists view other dimensions of life as equally significant. Freud, for example, believed that it was work and love that gave us our sense of meaning; others would add faith to that. While I don't dispute these, I'm aware of the dangers that arise when people become too dependent on others to supply their sense of meaning rather than finding it, or taking responsibility for it, within themselves.

I am at heart a pragmatist, however, not a psychologist, which might go some way to explaining why I dwell on a practical expression of meaning through work rather than through more ethereal aspects. As someone with a strong personal faith and a positive experience of love, I certainly don't intend to diminish the value of these in our lives. Even if you feel strongly that your own sense of meaning and purpose comes from elements other than work, I would contend that they are not complete unless expressed vocationally. For that to happen requires a degree of personal insight and understanding about yourself that I hope this book will go some way towards enabling.

I know from the work I do with my clients just how many people who buy personal development books neither complete the exercises nor act on them. Reading this book will make little difference to your search for a more meaningful working life if it doesn't lead to action. The real learning will come from the steps you take. It is the combination of reading and action that will lead to growth. As Ernest Hemingway rather mischievously wrote in *Death in the Afternoon*, 'There are two sorts of guide books; those that are read before and those that are to be read after and the ones that are to be read after the fact are bound to be incomprehensible to a certain extent before; if the fact is of enough importance in itself. So with any book on mountain ski-ing, sexual intercourse, wing shooting, or any other thing which it is impossible to make come true on paper, or at least impossible to attempt to make more than one version of at a time on paper, it being always an individual experience, there comes a place in the guide book where you must say do not come back until you have ski-ed, had sexual intercourse, shot quail or grouse, or been to the bullfight so that you will know what we are talking about.' Keep this in mind as you read *Why Do I Do This Every Day?* – but be assured I use much shorter sentences.

Many people gave me their support, encouragement and ideas while I was writing and helped to strengthen the content as a result. Any shortcomings are down to me. I would especially like to thank: John Anderson, Michael Cook, Meryl Doney, Colin Dyer, Daren Felgate, Rob Francis, Fiona Hall, Rob Jackson, Ursula Jost, Dr Nick King, Mark Kokocki, Steve Lawson, Alison Lyon, Nicky Martin, Lewis Milligan, Adrian Pearson, Judy Reith, Helen Walton, Olivia Warburton, Martin Wroe, my family, and Morag Reeve and the team at Lion Hudson.

Many clients from my coaching practice helped to inspire me with their stories, experiences and insights and the book truly would not have been possible without them. Some of their stories are here, although I have changed identities and details to preserve confidentiality – in some cases I have blended the experiences of more than one person into an anecdote in order to strengthen the narrative and draw attention away from any one individual.

My particular thanks to John Bailey whose help and support was unstinting at all times during the writing of this book. He made his computer available to me when my own broke down and took forever to be repaired. He also orchestrated a house move during the final weeks of writing; and gave so much more than I had any right to expect. I've yet to find a way to thank him adequately.

Fraser Dyer
London, October 2004

One: The causes of career disaffection

I caught up with an old friend on the phone recently and told her I was writing a book for people who want a meaningful working life. 'It's funny you should mention that,' she said. 'A former colleague of mine was just talking about exactly that issue. She'd been sent on a professional development course by her employer. When she turned up there were twenty other women sitting around the room wondering where their lives were going and why they were so unhappy in their jobs.'

I wasn't surprised. It is a characteristic of today's workforce that so many people feel they still don't know what they want to be when they grow up. At the centre of the issue is a concern that something significant is missing from their experience of work. For those affected, there is a growing anxiety about being trapped in an unfulfilling career or profession for the remainder of their working lives.

Of course, lots of us moan about our jobs. We've been doing so since the industrial revolution. This crisis, however, goes beyond the usual 'I hate my boss' or 'you won't believe how stressed I am' conversations that are familiar to many of us from listening to friends and colleagues. It cuts to the heart of those affected because the significance of their work and their sense of purpose is being challenged. When they look at their career expectations and compare them to the reality, there is an overwhelming sense of disappointment. They thought it would be better than this.

Before looking at some of the factors that have contributed to creating career disaffection in today's workforce, it is important to see the wider context. It is not the case that a whole generation feels trapped or disillusioned about their work. Some have successfully chosen – or landed in – jobs that suit them well where stability and opportunities for advancement are available. Nor is everyone looking for the same experience from their work. Your individual personality and character determine, in part, what will make a motivating and rewarding occupation for you. We neither all share the same expectations about work nor have the same levels of tolerance for factors that create disaffection.

So, in laying out the reasons for people's sense of crisis around their work, I am by no means suggesting that these are shared by everyone or even that they are common to all who feel disaffected. What I am attempting to do is describe the most common themes that arise when listening to people express unhappiness about their experience of work. If they are not shared by you it makes them no less real for others and, collectively, I hope they help to explain why so many people feel confused and dismayed by the direction of their career.

■ The problem with careers advice

For many the problems started before they left school. Here's a sentence you don't often hear: 'We had really *great* careers advisers at our school.'

For a long time, careers guidance was another cog in the wheel of processed education. It felt to some that it was less about their fulfilment and more about getting them off the school's hands and into the workforce as efficiently as possible. I heard an interview on the radio recently with a man who had grown up in a mining community. When he sat down with his careers adviser he was asked only one question: 'Which colliery do your father and brothers work in?' When the pupil answered, the adviser replied, 'We'll put you down for that one then,' and moved on to the next pupil.

And here's the problem. How are adolescents supposed to make big career decisions at a time when not only is their experience of life and work extremely limited but their hormones are wreaking so much havoc that rational thought is sometimes barely possible? With no experience of work to go on, young people have very little data from which to draw conclusions. My notions of work as a sixteen-year-old were hardly more advanced than at eight when I got a doctor's kit for Christmas and thought that would be a nice job because you got a stethoscope and a jar of tongue depressors. It's hardly the basis on which to build a vocation.

Today's generation of disaffected workers relied on the guidance of parents, teachers and careers advisers that veered towards a safe and sensible approach to building a career. I hear many stories from people who were dissuaded from following their interests or talents and sold out to a safe – but ultimately uninspiring – career choice. Others made opportunistic choices based on what was available to them. As one school teacher said to me, 'I see pupils who get straight As go on to do medicine and law because they can – not because they're interested.'

One person who was talked out of her first choice is Grace. She developed an interest in Arabic history and culture while at school and decided to pursue a university course in Arabic Studies. Well-meaning adults who thought she should study a more practical subject talked her out of it and she took languages instead. Now in her early forties, Grace is bored by her current work and feels despondent about spending another twenty-odd years plodding away at an unfulfilling occupation. She still dreams of work in North Africa or the Middle East and regrets not being more determined about taking the university course of her choice but feels (mistakenly in my view) it is now too late to do anything about it.

The sensible advice of well-meaning adults is motivated from the best of places – a desire to see their children or pupils succeed. Indeed, adults possess the very life and work experience that young people lack to help them make informed choices so it is inevitable that they will provide important insights when young people are making key decisions.

When today's workers were leaving school, this guidance wasn't always helpful. Although many still had no clue as to what line of work to pursue, others, like Grace, did have an inkling of where their interests lay. Fragile ambitions to pursue cultural or historic interests, nurture creative or artistic talents or simply think on a bigger scale were often crushed by elders who knew better. Instead of being encouraged to listen to their intuition, many school leavers were taught to be realistic and practical and to scale down their ambitions to something safe and sensible.

It is not that the adults' advice was bad, just that it was out of date. A major generational shift was occurring between adults who had grown up in a country reconstructing itself after a war and their children who saw the world very differently. While adults understandably wanted to enable their children to grasp opportunities they themselves had never had, the children took those same opportunities for granted and were thinking beyond them. Where the adults grew up in an environment of danger, disease and food shortages and wanted to protect their children from experiencing that, the children felt safe, healthy and well provided for.

That kind of stability was the norm for my generation and it bred a sense of possibility that went beyond the conventional and safe careers that our parents and teachers thought we should embrace. Where they wanted us to be, perhaps, engineers, accountants, nurses and bank managers, we aspired to be astronauts, TV presenters, rock stars and such. Little wonder so many living rooms of the 1970s were ablaze with arguments. The adults in our lives never realized how successful they had been in creating a safe and prosperous Britain in which our dreams could flourish. Their ambitions for us were often driven by their fears; our own dreams were fuelled by the possibilities we saw around us. Where they saw us as being reckless with the security they had provided, we could take that stability for granted and build towering hopes upon it. We saw glittering new work opportunities in the media, arts or abroad where they saw flash-in-the-pan trends that embodied the very uncertainties and unpredictability they had worked hard to eliminate for us. We can hardly blame them.

Today's generation grew up with high expectations of what their careers would offer them and this is the key to the disillusionment that so many people feel today. The expectations and possibilities that were entertained, however fleetingly, in their youth have not yet been realized. And while a place in university was more possible than before, and exciting new areas of work existed, the experience that their working lives were to deliver contained some shocks.

■ The culture of overwork

Rachel is 35 years old and a human rights lawyer. She earned just over £60,000 working for a specialist firm based in Manchester. Her job tapped into a long-held passion she had for justice and she knew that the work she was doing meant that her disempowered and exploited clients would get a fairer deal. What could be more rewarding? Not only did the job pay handsomely but it also connected to her personal values and she could see the difference her work made. Her parents were also very proud of her and what she had achieved.

In reality, though, Rachel's working life had been a misery for several years. She was working a 60-hour week at the office, then taking more work home with her at the weekend. She permanently felt stressed and exhausted and had little time for a social life. She particularly resented this because she was single and had no time or opportunity to meet new men. As a result of her exhaustion, mistakes and oversights were beginning to creep into her work about which her boss gave her a really hard time. When she told him she was finding it difficult to keep on top of the workload, he said that if she couldn't stand the heat she should get out of the kitchen. He increased her client load and told her to improve her work or he would implement the firm's disciplinary procedure.

When I first met Rachel, she wasn't prepared to give up on law, not least because of pressure from her family and friends. If ever she talked about looking for a new career, they would remind her of all the reasons why this was a really stupid idea. Given how fatigued she was, Rachel decided to take a break, so resigned from her job and went on a long holiday to reflect on what she wanted to do next. I got a postcard from Peru saying she was having a great time and was feeling greatly rested and rejuvenated.

When she returned to the UK, Rachel secured another post with a law firm working on similar cases. It was only a few months later that I got a call from her asking to come and see me when she was next in London. I opened the door to the old Rachel – stressed, exhausted and deeply unhappy. A similar scenario had played itself out in her new firm as in the old and the workload was breaking her. Her new boss was again unsympathetic and made it clear that if she wasn't prepared to work the long hours required to keep on top of the case load, she wouldn't be getting a good reference from the firm.

Having quickly reached a state of feeling worn out again, Rachel also realized that she just didn't have the time or energy to be able to think clearly about what she wanted to do next. She was beginning to realize that maybe law wasn't the career for her and felt sure there was something else out there that would deliver the quality of working life and personal fulfilment she desired.

Rachel's feelings of frustration with her work are not unique. What is so disheartening about her story is that here was someone who had succeeded in qualifying in a highly desirable profession and had found a branch of it that resonated strongly with her personal values and interests. In spite of this, the poor quality of her working life did not make these benefits worthwhile.

The pressure on workers to put in longer hours is putting a greater strain on us than ever. In her book, *Willing Slaves: How the Overwork Culture is Ruling Our Lives*, journalist Madeleine Bunting writes:

Britain's full-time workers put in the longest hours in Europe at 43.6 a week, well ahead of the EU average of 40.3. These figures conceal the increasing polarisation of work between those who have none (16.4 per cent of households have no one in work) and those who have too much. The figure is rising: between 1998 and 2003 British workers put in an extra 0.7 hours a week on average; but this masks the full scale of the accelerating trend of the overwork culture. The number working more than forty-eight hours has more than doubled since 1998, from 10 per cent to 26 per cent. Another survey tracked how the number working more than sixty hours a week is shooting up. Between 2000 and 2002 it leapt by a third, to one in six of all workers, so that a fifth of thirty- to thirty-nine-year-olds are working over sixty hours – a critical proportion of those likely to be at a pivotal point in beginning their own families, and well ahead of any other European country.

The more you scrutinize the figures, the worse it gets. 'Since 1992 the number of women working more than forty-eight hours a week has increased by a staggering 52 per cent, and the proportion working over sixty hours has more than doubled, from 6 per cent to 13 per cent – one in eight of the female workforce. Long hours is no longer solely a male disease.'

But what about the rewards for working so hard? If you demonstrate your loyalty, devotion and commitment to your job, your employer will surely be keen to hold on to you and reward you with rapid promotion and a healthy pension. Right?

■ Eroded loyalty of employers

The boom and bust years of the 1980s and early 1990s eroded the loyalty of employers towards their staff. Where once workers could reasonably expect a career for life, often within the same firm, now employers shed them swiftly at the first sign of an economic downturn. Some people went through the cycle of redundancy several times as big businesses downsized in order to stay afloat in choppy economic conditions.

This was particularly rough for those nearing retirement who were laid off before they could collect on their pensions yet were regarded as 'too old' by employers elsewhere. Younger workers watched on as employers dumped costlier, older staff in favour of retaining younger and less expensive employees. While not threatened directly by this, younger employees started to wonder seriously about the loyalty of their company.

With growing unease, it became clear to many people that businesses felt their staff were easily dispensable and not worth investing in. Some began to wonder why they should show loyalty and commitment to their employer if it wasn't going to be returned. While they understood that companies had a commitment to their shareholders or funders, they didn't feel that employees deserved the sometimes bloody-minded treatment they received. For those who held on to their jobs, life wasn't always easy either. One of the ways that employers coped with the shift in workload caused by redundancy was to pile more work on to remaining staff.

Andy is a typical example. When he was working as Marketing Manager in a mid-sized company, his bosses cut his departmental staffing budget on two occasions. While they were fortunate to achieve this through voluntary redundancy and natural wastage, the work that the departing staff undertook did not leave the company alongside them. Andy ended up absorbing the work of one team member and, later, part of another. 'I have two and a half jobs,' he says. 'The directors told me they would sort it out through an "infrastructure review" but when the dust settled nothing had changed. Except they had increased my responsibilities.'

Grateful to still be in a job in spite of the considerable pressure he's under, Andy is ten years away from the earliest age at which he can retire. He's hoping to cling on to his job until then but doesn't always feel optimistic about this possibility and wonders if he should leave now while there is still time to make a go of a new job elsewhere. 'It's a tough decision to make. Do I motor along here until I can retire, not certain there will always be a job for me, or try to get a new job knowing that employers want younger staff who they perceive as more cutting edge?' In short, he feels that his experience isn't valued elsewhere but he also knows it won't count for much in his existing company if they experience any more tough times. In the meantime, he has to cope with the stress and long hours of doing two and a half jobs.

■ Rapid pace of change

Along with a sense of eroded loyalty from employers, many workers have to cope with constant changes. Teachers are particularly well known for having had repeatedly to deal with changes to the curriculum, methods of testing, policies and procedures, not to mention expanding paperwork and bureaucracy. I know teachers who have been in post for twenty years and say they don't feel they have settled into the job yet. Just as they get used to the latest ways of doing things, the government or education authority launch another new initiative. Such is the frustration at this constant meddling that many have left the profession feeling despondent that their vocation turned sour.

If certain public sector workers feel that they are struggling to keep pace with change, their private sector colleagues can certainly empathize. The rate of technological advancement is now so fast that businesses need to be able to deal with changes in the market as swiftly as possible. If you've ever bought a computer you'll be familiar with the frustration of seeing the price of it plummet shortly afterwards because it has become laughably obsolete already. As soon as one company enhances a product with better speed or performance, all of its competitors must adapt swiftly to survive. This cut and thrust is what makes commerce attractive to some people.

I believe today's workers are better able to deal with change if it is managed well. It is not an unwillingness to adapt that makes change stressful for people but the change management process when it is handled clumsily or is badly communicated. When staff are pushed around without clearly understanding what they are supposed to be doing now (or why), or without being given the resources to fulfil their new role, then stress is inevitable. And a significant cause of career disaffection is when people have gone through change mismanagement one time too often.

This is no more apparent than in the case of management fads: when the boss returns from holiday having read his favourite business guru's latest Big Idea and starts trying to implement it; or calls in the consultants to sharpen up the company's performance.

Remember Total Quality Management? Or Business Process Re-engineering? With the kind of brash overconfidence more normally seen in adverts for washing powder, each of these was sold to businesses as the best way to organize your company – until the next one came along, claiming to be even better. Managers often like new theories because they can help to simplify a way of understanding and managing a very complicated issue. But in the way that no washing powder gets rid of every stain, no management fad fully delivers what it promises in theory.

Yet managers convert to them with evangelical zeal, confident that they are really going to shake out all the company's problems and set them on the path to glory. Frontline workers again bear the brunt of this chopping and changing where their needs and insights are swept aside in pursuit of the latest dogma. Indeed, one of the developers of 're-engineering' conceded that his particular approach to business management had focused on profitability and efficiency while overlooking the people element, which he later admitted was crucial.

Workers who were left to watch passively the implementation of a management fad from the sidelines were often in a good position to advise on where and how the implementation would and wouldn't work. Yet they were never asked. Managers who were too quick to listen solely to consultants and not enough to their own internal experts implemented schemes over the heads of staff who could only resign themselves to the blunders being made.

■ Lack of recognition

This failure by managers to acknowledge and value their staff's expertise and insight is another contributory factor to the disaffection of workers. They just don't feel listened to, even when they have much of value to say to the company.

Angela ran the mail order gift catalogue for a well-known art gallery. After she had been a couple of years in the post, sales began to fall. Angela knew that this was part of a wider trend linked to an economic downturn. Through a professional association to which she belonged, she discovered that her colleagues running other gallery, museum or charity catalogues were experiencing a similar percentage drop in sales. Given that she had over a decade's experience in the field with different institutions, Angela was easily able to put together a plan for reducing overheads and stimulating new sales.

Her boss saw things differently. He decided to hire one of the country's leading consultants in mail order sales to advise on what they should do. The consultant ran a review of the business then met with Angela and her boss to present his recommendations. He suggested cutting overheads and stimulating new sales in exactly the way Angela had advised. This time, however, her boss was eager to listen and agree to the strategy. At one point when they were alone, the consultant turned to Angela and said that he realized that he was only telling the gallery what Angela had already recommended and he couldn't understand why they wouldn't listen to her. Strangely enough, neither could she.

Perhaps it's a case of prophets having no honour in their home town, but many employees feel their knowledge and experience is disregarded in favour of that of managers and consultants. Just this week a friend told me of a new management system being proposed in his workplace. In this case, the managers and consultants had met with key staff, the latter patiently explaining over a period of weeks why the proposed system wouldn't work. Eventually the management sent out an email explaining the scheme was being dropped because the consultants had decided it was unworkable. Despite the fact it was staff who had shed light on the problems inherent in the proposal, the infallibility of the consultants was preserved to the end. The email also failed to mention that the cost of this exercise to the company was in the region of £150,000.

■ Bureaucratization of the workplace

It is not only the attitude of managers that can leave employees feeling undervalued at work. Modern recruitment and employment practices have a built-in tendency to dehumanize individuals, as accountants and human resources personnel become ever more obsessed with counting, measuring and regulating.

It tells us something about the problem that the phrase 'human resources' was coined in the first place. No longer are you the driving force of your company's work and success or the living, breathing heart of its operation. You are just another resource alongside finances, facilities and fixtures and fittings. The work of what used to be called 'Personnel' is not (as many new employees naively assume but of which they are swiftly disabused) about taking care of the needs and interest of staff. It's about making sure that the company gets the most bangs for its buck out of you. HR departments too often – though not always – become like finance departments where the currency is people rather than pennies.

In *Be Your Own Career Consultant*, Gary Pyke and Stuart Neath (themselves career development consultants) explain why human resources departments no longer take an interest in helping employees develop their careers. 'They have gone the way of many other departments: measured on the number of transactions they perform, the price they can get for a training course (the cheaper the better) and what they cost as an overhead compared to the investment in them (again, the cheaper the better).'

Often incapable of making any decisions unless first there is a yard of policy in place, HR departments have become professional fundamentalists, scanning their sacred documents to see whether or not it is permissible for them to accommodate your individual needs and career aspirations. Heaven forbid that you should have a life and responsibilities outside work that occasionally impinge on your working hours. Compassion has been documented and filed under 'P' for policy. Many workers today feel that the soul is being squeezed out of the workplace because there are too many inflexible procedures and systems that fail to take account of staff individuality.

There are, of course, good people in the HR profession too, people who see the limitations of bureaucratization in the workplace and the negative impact it has on the motivation of individuals. They often share the frustration their colleagues have of not being given enough of a voice, or of their expertise not being called upon, in the management of people. They are merely expected to implement decisions made by the 'experts' at the top of the hierarchy.

It is the case elsewhere, however, that HR staff are informing the decisions that executives make and which contribute to making employment so impersonal, regulated and policy-heavy that staff efforts to give their best to their work are stifled. People don't feel trusted when they are locked into a rigid system of rules and regulations, and you meddle with employee trust at your peril. Little wonder one in eight working adults are now self-employed. Workers are gasping for air in a culture of work that suffocates their capacity to fulfil their potential or meet their deepest motivational needs.

People need room to stretch their wings on the job. They want opportunities to grow and develop and learn, and for the job to adapt around their strengths, skills and interests. They want to be able to use their initiative, not be told to refer anything out of the ordinary to a supervisor.

The development of the McJob – where people are no more than a cog in a highly mechanized system – is de-skilling and dehumanizing. Whether in fast food joints, call centres, financial institutions, shops, business, manufacturing or industry, employers who see people only as a pair of hands or a mouthpiece are contributing to the current career crisis (and, incidentally, undermining the quality of customer service).

While there are obviously people who are suited to working in this kind of way, I'm not sure it is as many as some employers would have us believe. People like working where they can think and use their initiative. They want to help customers and clients solve their problems. The *can't-do* culture at work, created by computer systems which can only perform a limited number of predetermined routines, is as frustrating for staff as it is for customers.

A number of years ago, when my friend Adrian wanted to get a new phone line installed, he encountered the impact this *can't-do* culture can have on employees. Adrian was a home-based freelance worker but his small office at home was suddenly needed to accommodate the baby, the deal on a new house that he and his wife were buying having abruptly fallen through. He needed to relocate his office within a week. Frantic searching revealed an office not far away. As his work involved a number of time-critical projects, he needed two telephone lines to be installed at extremely short notice. So he rang the telephone company. The customer services adviser he spoke to said that they would post out a form which, once Adrian had completed and returned it, would enable them to schedule an installation date. Adrian explained the urgency for getting the lines installed and that the time involved in posting out the form, receiving it, filling it out and posting it back would create too much of a delay. Knowing that the telephone company's office was nearby, he asked if he couldn't go then and there and fill out the form in person? 'I'm sorry sir but we're not able to do that for you,' he was told. 'The system won't allow it.'

Adrian, a stubborn man and not easily put off, stressed again the urgency with which he needed his new lines but the young man said there was nothing he could do other than put the form in the post. Adrian's last gambit was to appeal to the lad's personal motivation. 'Wouldn't it make you feel good to know at the end of the day that you had really made a difference to somebody? That you'd been able to use your initiative and solve a problem that the system can't deal with?' But nothing would budge the adviser from his set responses so Adrian rang off feeling despondent. However, after twenty minutes the phone rang and the same customer adviser, breathless with excitement, said that he'd thought about what Adrian had said and, yes, he could do it and it would make him feel great that he'd achieved something special for someone. 'Tell you what,' the adviser said, 'I'm on a break at 3 o'clock. I'll meet you in reception and bring the paperwork with me so that you can fill it out immediately. And I have already scheduled your line installation for this Thursday morning.'

When he and Adrian met, the customer services adviser was indeed happy to help and glad that he'd been able to resolve Adrian's problem. I'm not surprised. In service jobs it is so much more rewarding and builds better relationships with customers to be able to say 'Yes, I can do that' than to tell them it's not possible. Finding a way of working around the system to give the customer the solution needed was what made working in customer services rewarding for me nearly twenty years ago. The system worked well for about 90 per cent of people while the others continually surprised us with requests that the system designers had never anticipated. So we worked out ways of bypassing the system, and I spent many hours rummaging through piles of order forms to manually delete an item on it, or tracking down an order on the packing floor to slip an extra item in. In those days – as a poster on my manager's wall reminded us – the customer was king. These days the customer is often made to feel unwelcome if they need something done that stands outside the pre-programmed procedures on the computer.

Adrian's tale, sadly, has a nasty sting in it. On the day his phone lines were due to be installed, no engineers turned up at his house. He rang the telephone people but wasn't able to reach the young man who'd helped him out previously. Eventually he got through to the supervisor. He began to outline his story before being interrupted. 'Oh, it's you,' she said. 'Have you any idea of the trouble you've caused? The person who helped you with your little stunt has been demoted. And as for you,' she added vindictively, 'I've put your order to the back of the queue. You'll just have to wait your turn.'

These kinds of over-structured and procedure-driven jobs can treat employees (and sometimes customers) as if they aren't very bright. Yet it is simply not the case that the people doing these kinds of service roles aren't intelligent. In fact, many of them are graduates. In March 2004, two leading political economists produced a report showing that, three years after graduating, 40 per cent of recent graduates are in jobs that do not require degree-level skills.

This is worrying as it suggests that career disaffection is simply going to increase. If people have graduated they of course expect to be doing something more stimulating than flipping burgers, processing data or sitting in a call centre.

■ Lack of variety

It is not merely employees in low-skilled jobs who feel pigeonholed. Many of the disaffected – at all levels of the career ladder – talk about lack of variety in their work. They feel locked into a particular role and function where tasks and activities tend to be very similar from day to day. This is the upshot of both the way jobs are designed and the structure of organizations and is especially prevalent among old-fashioned employers who cling to hierarchical models of management. There is limited scope for managers to recognize the particular talents and abilities of individuals and develop the job around them.

Often the opposite is true: workers are expected to fit into tightly defined job descriptions that take no account of their individuality. The assumption behind this is that the organization has worked out the best way of fulfilling its own needs and has identified the required tasks and activities that different role-holders must undertake to keep the whole organization functioning smoothly and efficiently.

It is the words *smoothly and efficiently* that are the giveaway here. The notion that the organization is a tightly run and close-knit community of workers, where individuals each occupy a particular function that dovetails beautifully with everyone else's, is very far removed from the experience of most. A more typical scenario is a daily encounter with miscommunication, conflicting internal objectives, competitive and undermining behaviour between departments, endless meetings to untangle the confusion and enough bureaucracy to make the civil service look streamlined.

Keeping staff in tightly defined roles becomes the managers' way of kidding themselves that they are exercising some control over this circus. And staff who wish to grow and develop on the job find it hard to see why they must be constrained within their role because they see through the myth that the organization is functioning like clockwork. People see ways of using their skills and abilities to provide solutions to some of the problems being encountered or to identify new ways of doing things that would improve effectiveness. So when they are held back from doing this by insecure or controlling managers, the frustration is understandable. Not only do employees feel that their skills and experience are being undervalued but they have to continue to live with problems to which they can see a solution.

Some occupations obviously rely heavily on people fulfilling their jobs in exactly the same way every day. In some sectors of manufacturing or construction, for example, it wouldn't do for people to start getting creative on the job. But in Britain today an increasing number of people are occupied in service roles, working for organizations that are responsible for delivering products, support, services or advice to customers. Here there is much more scope for flexibility of roles. The frequency with which some organizations get restructured is evidence of this flexibility: there is more than one way for work to be accomplished.

Yet in between the upheaval of reorganizing the infrastructure of the business and redefining the tasks that people do, the business is locked down again into rigid functions.

■ No tangible outcomes

If a lack of both flexibility and recognition is disheartening to some people, so too is the lack of a tangible outcome to their work. A common frustration I hear from people is that their work leads to nothing visible and concrete. They like to see the results of their labours. If you build a car, design a building, write a book, craft some furniture, fill a dental cavity or even a hole in the road, you can at least see the difference you've made. There is something physical that you can touch and say 'I helped to make that'. And those who work with people – teaching, healing, caring, advising – can often see the difference they've made in the lives of others.

Yet many people work in process jobs. That is to say, they are part of a chain of work that leads to an outcome that may not be seen by them. They sit in front of computers all day or are on the telephone. Perhaps they monitor the work of others or move products about. Often much of the thinking is done for them in the way that cash registers not only do all the sums for the operator but can now also tell them what to say to customers.

This approach to work doesn't sit well with the basic human need to be productive. For those who want to get back to basics and create, grow, cook, craft or produce, many of the jobs in today's workplace can only fail to satisfy. Clients show me their hands saying they want to do something with them. They want dirt under their fingernails or calluses on their palms. They want to connect the use of their hands with the imagination of their minds and create something new. They want to be outdoors using muscles in all parts of their bodies, not simply watching their bottoms slowly spread ever fatter over the edge of a cheap swivel chair.

For some of the disaffected, there is a resurgence of something quite primal in the needs they want to fulfil. Often the process jobs they are doing are the antithesis of that desire. What people often struggle with is finding a way out of situations where job design, management practices and business fads have contributed to undermining their sense of fulfilment and satisfaction at work. If one has worked in a particular industry or profession since leaving school or university, it can be a fairly radical decision to switch to another career altogether. People don't want to risk having to start at the bottom of the ladder again and, as time progresses, understandably want to advance in terms of responsibility and earnings. So the only way is up, gaining promotion within their existing job or profession.

■ The management trap

This brings us to another factor that leads to career disaffection – it is the management trap. Actually, management posts are full of paradoxes and contradictions but for the disaffected the main one is that their promotion can put them out of touch with a job they loved.

By moving into a managerial role, which they see as the only way to advance, some workers find that they have to leave behind the kind of tasks, relationships and activities that made their job rewarding in the first place. Suddenly less time is spent on the hands-on work they used to do and more of it is taken up with meetings, people management and paperwork. While a promotion into management may be seen as advancement in terms of income, responsibility and job security (don't bet on it), it can also detract from fulfilment. Yet everyone knows it's a bad career strategy not to be seen to be advancing. A lot of stock is placed on employees' hunger for promotion. Carrying on doing a job we love is somehow seen to be a failure. Hang on: who are the real losers here?

And it's not just moving away from enjoyable work that causes the management trap. Many people often feel ill-equipped and lacking in the necessary skills to take on a management position, so their confidence is undermined. Rather than feeling self-assured and competent in the job, a management move can cause severe stress and low self-esteem.

This may not be false modesty on the part of new managers. Too often they really *are* ill-equipped to take on a management role. Workplace logic says that if you are good at, say, dealing with customers, then you'll be equally good at managing others to deal with customers. As the two roles are so very different, how does anyone figure that if you can do one you are automatically skilled in the other?

Of course some people relish management jobs – they really do want to move up. But, for the rest, why isn't enjoying one's job seen as an achievement? Professional development is seen in a different light when people are rewarded for their experience and given greater flexibility to adapt their job as they grow into it. There are sometimes more ways to evolve a job than upwards but for many that opportunity doesn't exist. The management trap is the choice to stay put and lose the respect of those around you or move up into a job you won't enjoy and will get stressed about.

■ Unfulfilled potential

This factor again prompts some to seek new directions for their career, take on retraining or move into self-employment. Doing work that is intrinsically enjoyable is one of the keys to a fulfilling occupation. There is something about the tasks and activities involved in the job that the worker finds rewarding and satisfying. They may not even be able to explain why they like it but it simply suits them down to the ground.

These enjoyable tasks are often things that the person is naturally good at. There seems to be a clear link between talent and enjoyment. Sometimes a natural ability still needs to be trained – such as musical, technical or linguistic skills – but the best in those areas usually have natural talent to begin with. When we get to use our built-in abilities, it is a deeply satisfying experience.

The fortunate ones are those whose abilities were spotted and nurtured early on. Many of those who are leaders in their field had opportunities to grow their talent while still at school. For others, that opportunity wasn't there and they have followed a career path that seemed sensible or was based on available opportunities rather than making the most of who they were as an individual. For some of the disaffected this is at the hub of their frustration with their career. They just don't feel they are making the most of themselves or fulfilling their potential.

One such person is Karen. Karen was educated in Belfast, both at school and university. On the advice of her elders and betters, she did a maths degree although she really wanted to pursue a career in investment management. On graduating, she started to train as an actuary with an insurance company but, having already had so many years in education, she didn't really want to spend more time studying for professional qualifications. It was time to start living. So she switched tracks and became an insurance broker instead. Although it was a career move that was easy to make at the time, it took her even further away from her original ambition. She ended up working for a dominating and controlling boss and, although she knew the job was not good for her, she felt trapped and unable to move on. 'I felt like a rabbit caught in the glare of headlights,' she told me. 'I knew I needed to make a move but I was so afraid of getting it wrong that I stayed put for longer than I should have.'

Eventually, the stress and frustration was so intense it prompted her resignation. She moved to a large financial services company and became responsible for managing a sales team. This felt like a positive career move. It meant Karen got out of the stressful situation she was in, gained a promotion and moved into a field of work that she'd been told she would do well in – when she'd been at university she'd undertaken a psychometric test which told her she was predisposed to working in sales.

She says she pretty much enjoys this new job, for which she receives a reasonable salary plus some good bonuses. Yet Karen feels that she took a wrong turn somewhere. 'I'm not really a sales person at all. It's not what I want, it doesn't use many of the technical skills I have and I worry about the pressure of meeting targets. And customers don't trust our profession as much as they once did, which makes selling harder.'

Although only 40, Karen says she's missed the boat. 'I'd love a complete change of lifestyle and a chance to move into work that feels like it's more suited to who I am as a person. But I tell myself, "You've had your chance. You are 40 now and it's too late to do anything about it." '

This sense of feeling duty-bound to live with the decisions of the past is very common among those who are disaffected with their career. In fact, there is no reason why Karen couldn't make a successful career move at forty when there is still plenty of time and energy to apply to it. But like many others, she finds it difficult to face the disruption and uncertainty that this would cause.

A sense of loyalty to employers and profession, as well as family commitments, contributes to a tendency to maintain the status quo. People like Karen also share her sense that their work isn't really about them but has been heavily shaped by those around them. Whether through following direct advice, the results of psychometric tests or simply falling into whatever convenient opportunities are presented to them, many workers feel that they are ill-matched to the career they are in. By letting the needs of others (in the main, employers) determine their choices and the direction their careers take, today's workers have not learned to take their own needs seriously when making decisions about their occupation.

Since school, we have had to prove ourselves to others. The big question we all grew up with was 'Are you good enough?' Good enough to take the subjects you want at school? Good enough to gain a pass in your exams? Good enough to get a place on the university or training course of your choice?

And, of course, when it comes to applying for jobs the whole emphasis is on whether we have what it takes to satisfy the employer. The selection and interviewing process is heavily biased towards the needs of the employer and involves measuring candidates against those criteria. Of course employers need to be sure that new staff are up to the job, but if people are to be fulfilled and motivated in those posts then workers' needs must also be met. The problem has been that not enough emphasis or opportunity is put on exploring a potential employee's career aims. From the point of view of many workers, little space is given to this important piece of the occupational jigsaw.

■ Taking responsibility for your career

It is not universally the case that potential employees' career aims are not taken into account. In some job sectors employees are expected to have a clear idea of their own career aims and to negotiate with prospective employers on the content of their job to ensure it satisfies the objectives of *both* parties. Elsewhere, however, especially within larger more bureaucratic organizations, the process is driven by employers who 'design' jobs, expecting prospective candidates to prove their ability to do them. There is an unwritten assumption that the employer's needs are more important than yours, or perhaps that they are clever enough to design such an attractive job that simply by applying for it you have indicated that your own needs will be satisfied in full if offered the post.

Satisfying the 'good enough' question has meant that many have become conditioned to seeing themselves *only* with regard to how well they measure up to the requirements of others – whether teachers, parents or employers.

In truth, no matter what you want to do for a living, you will always be required to do something which meets the needs of somebody else, whether employer, client or customer. A successful career is about being able to deliver products and services that others desire. So there is no question that taking account of the needs of whoever pays for your work is vital. It is just that the balance of needs must be properly adjusted so that both worker and employer get what they want from the process. This clearly requires workers to take some responsibility for their own career aims and, in fairness to employers, not all staff think in this way. Some see their occupation as just a job and aim to squeeze as much money out of their employer for the least effort. There is no aspirational contract between staff and employer in these situations. The company just wants a pair of hands and the workers just want to get home with as much money and as little exhaustion as possible. Their career aims extend no further than that.

Sadly this is most often evidenced in poorly paid jobs. As we shall see later, it is the more affluent who can afford to begin thinking about their own personal fulfilment. When money is tight, just hanging onto a job and putting food on the table is as far as many people's aspirations extend. And employers will sometimes take advantage of the power this gives them. Beggars really cannot be choosers.

But this doesn't explain why the better off sometimes fail to take their own needs seriously and continue to let employers control their career paths and choices. And if they've not started off with a clear idea of where they want their work to go, it is easy for them to eventually lose touch completely with any understanding of what kind of work would satisfy them. So they experience uneasiness about their working life that they cannot articulate. They know they are not fulfilled but they are not equipped with the mindset or tools to help them think differently about their work.

Often when I work with clients on career issues, a good deal of time is spent trying to get them to think differently about themselves in relation to work. They begin to think about what is important to them that would make their work enjoyable and rewarding. It is testimony to the extent to which we have become so used to thinking of ourselves in relation to the needs of others that some people find this extremely difficult. If someone has been working for twenty years and all that time has been spent measuring themselves against others' requirements, decisions being based on what others perceive as their qualities (which then dictate what their work should be), of course people will lose their way. They simply lose touch with any real sense of their desires and aspirations.

Even for some of those who appear to be quite driven by ambition, it is often not their own personal ambition they are pursuing but rather the expected norm within their profession. That is to say, they have taken on board the collective ambition of their colleagues or place of work.

I experienced this collective drive at first hand in a brief and wholly undistinguished career in financial services. My colleagues were pushing themselves to make that extra sale in order to move up the next rung of the ladder. As there were big steps between each rung, a whole series of smaller incentives were set up to keep people focused on achieving more. Most commonly, these related to either earning enough money to get one's dream car or to generating enough of a bonus to earn a place at the annual conference – tantalizingly located in the Caribbean.

I had joined financial services because I thought it would be a nice change to do a job involving a suit and briefcase, and to be able to explain complex financial issues to eager customers. My drive therefore operated on a somewhat different basis (not to mention that it was based on a preposterous delusion). Yet it was presumed by all around me that I would buy into the collective ambition that was part of the culture of that organization and be compelled by incentives rather than by the nature of the work itself. When I failed to show much sympathy for my boss, who had slaved hard to be eligible for a company Porsche only to discover his golf clubs wouldn't fit in the boot, it was clearly time for me to move on.

That people need to be motivated to do a job they are being offered may seem patently obvious. However, not enough employers are taking time to help staff understand their career objectives. The rise of the psychometric test has further contributed to this process – employers do not feel they even need to ask candidates to think about their aspirations. They merely ask them to take a test that purports to identify whether applicants have the right temperament for the job.

This approach to recruitment is not only folly but inherently disrespectful to employees because it fails to try to understand who they really are or to fully integrate the objectives of the employer with the career aims of the worker. Instead, everybody is merely reduced to being a type who must demonstrate the required collection of qualifications and experience before being slotted into their allotted place in the organizational machine. Little wonder that so many employees do not feel cared for these days.

Yet it is not enough to blame the system. For many businesses and organizations, the changing culture of work has meant that they have had to work hard to adapt and survive. And while it is true that there is sometimes thoughtless and ill-considered behaviour on the part of managers, many of them also feel confused and disaffected.

No matter how employment is organized, or whatever work trends are in vogue, people will continue to feel constrained as long as they are waiting for somebody else – such as employers – to create the right opportunities and circumstances that meet their needs. In order to move forward, the starting point for any disaffected worker is to take personal responsibility for their working life. For some, this will involve thinking seriously about themselves, and their relationship to work, for the first time. They may need to challenge some well-ingrained conventions and assumptions about how to pursue a fulfilling career to gain a sense of their potential.

While the breakdown of the old career system may have caused confusion and disillusionment for some, the self-same changes have created new opportunities for those who are prepared to reach out for them. Indeed, it is arguable that there has never been a better time to rethink your career because the world of work provides greater opportunities than ever before to create a fulfilling and meaningful working life.

■ To think about...

1. What have been the highs and lows of your own career path? What were the key moments that helped you develop your career, and are there any workplace trends that particularly undermine your motivation and fulfilment?

2. If you could start your career over again, knowing what you know now, would you make any different decisions? If so, what?

3. To what extent have you taken responsibility for your career development, and are there moments when you could have been more proactive in making the choices you wanted?

4. Even wrong turns in your career can teach you much about yourself and the nature of meaningful work for you. Reflecting on your career to date – both positive and negative experiences – how would you summarize the lessons you've learned along the way?

Two: Why now is a great time to rethink your career

While the changes that have taken places in the workplace over the last twenty-five years have left some people feeling adrift with regard to their career, these same developments have created opportunities for others.

Not only has the economy of Britain changed but our attitudes to work and the choice of occupations available are also quite different from those of the late 1970s. While it is relatively easy to look back now and remember how different life was without the PC or the mobile phone, many of the factors that have created shifts in the landscape of work took place at such a slow and steady pace that many workers were barely conscious of the transition.

■ The service economy

This was not the case if you were, say, a steel worker, shipbuilder or worked on a production line. Employees in the manufacturing sector were all too aware that Britain's economy no longer relied on their skills, as factory after factory closed down, laying off, in some cases, near-whole communities of workers. Today Britain has a service economy, driven by the provision of information, communication, creativity and design. These days we sell what we *know* rather than what we *make*?

In London alone, art and design account for the city's second biggest source of income after financial services. Fashion, design, art and music are big business. And across the UK as a whole leisure, retail, communication and information services are the mainstay of the jobs market. Students looking for a summer job are more likely to end up processing data or making telephone calls than labouring on a building site or screwing caps onto widgets.

The rise in service-related occupations means that workers are selling their knowledge and skills to employers or, increasingly, to their own clients. As well as those services that businesses and other organizations can make use of, there is a second level of service provision that supports busy workers. With both partners out at work in seven out of ten households, there are plenty of people who need help in accomplishing all they have to do. Today's exhausted and busy workers require practical help with child care, domestic cleaning and gardening, as well as the physical and emotional support offered by personal trainers, complementary therapists, counsellors and coaches. And if you are so time-poor you can't even get round to copying your CDs onto your iPod, there is now an outfit that will do it for you, demonstrating that there is always room for entrepreneurs to spot a gap in the market.

Those who become self-employed require the help of other freelancers including accountants, IT support, virtual assistants, web-designers, copy-writers, business advisers and so on. It all adds up to a world of work where someone wants to buy the knowledge you have.

My own network of contacts, clients and acquaintances yields the following list of occupations (many undertaken on a freelance basis and/or based at home):

Accountant	Copy editor
Advertising creative	Copy writer
Architect	Corporate film-maker
Art conservator	Counsellor
Art dealer	Decorator
Carpenter	Design consultant
Child minder	Development officer
Composer	Dressmaker
Computer programmer	Educational tutor

Event organizer
Fitness trainer
Fundraiser
Gardener
Graphic designer
Hairdresser
Health adviser
Homeopath
Interior designer
Journalist
Landscape architect
Management consultant
Market analyst
Market researcher
Mechanic
Music teacher
Parenting coach
Personal assistant
Photographer

Policy adviser
PR consultant
Priest
Proofreader
Psychotherapist
Publicist
Quantity surveyor
Researcher
Shiatsu practitioner
Sound engineer
Solicitor
Sports coach
Stockbroker
Tax adviser
Tour operator
Training consultant
Urban planner
Web designer

Just from within my own sphere of contact, one can begin to see the diversity of ways in which people are selling their knowledge and talent. I may not know what they all do (development officer, anyone?) but I do know that they serve to illustrate how people are taking advantage of the changing culture of work.

■ The portability of work

Another impact of the emergence of the service economy is that work is no longer tied to one place. If you are manufacturing goods, then your workforce must come to where the resources are. If, like many people today, the key resources you require are a computer and a telephone then you can work virtually anywhere. The decentralization of the workplace now creates greater possibilities for people to balance the demands of their job with other priorities and responsibilities in their life – not least the family.

Affordable travel – particularly by air – means that workers are able to rethink where they live in relation to their work. If you don't have to be in the office every day and can work from home part of the time, it is now feasible to live further away, perhaps even in a different country. Workers in the south-east of England, for example, are now taking advantage of the Channel Tunnel and budget airlines to live in France and commute from there. One executive I know of flies from the UK to South Africa every Monday morning and returns on Thursday evening to be with his wife and family.

Employers are also taking advantage of these kinds of shifts to lower their overheads and increase their adaptability to rapidly changing markets. Rather than maintaining a team of experts on their payroll, they now hire freelancers in a vast range of fields and specialisms. There is no shortage of people willing to fulfil these functions. Moving into consultancy or freelance work has given many people greater autonomy and control over their work. And if organizations' reliance on freelancers is driven by a need for flexibility, that same requirement attracts workers into self-employment. Flexibility is now considered one of the most highly-prized perks in the workplace, as workers seek to spend more time with their families or in fulfilling their potential in other areas of life.

In Spring 2003, the government introduced flexible working rights which gave parents with young children the right to request flexible or part-time working arrangements from their employer. Plans are currently underway to extend this to employees who are caring for an elderly relative.

■ Flexible working

While freelancing can be the ultimate flexible job, people in employment increasingly have a range of options that allow them to get their work-life balance just right. Progressive-thinking employers now offer flexitime, sabbaticals, homeworking and hot-desking as ways of giving employees greater control and flexibility over their working life. Rather than getting too involved in what their staff do and when, work targets are agreed in terms of outcomes and then employees are left to work out how best they achieve these in the available time.

Jacqueline is someone who has taken advantage of these flexible arrangements to fulfil her potential. She is a software developer who spends her days in front of a computer terminal, developing new programmes for her company. She has worked with them for eight years and really enjoys her job. She likes having technical skills and knowledge that she can apply to her work and designing software also gives her an outlet for her creativity. On the down side, her work is quite isolated and static and, in spite of good working relationships with her colleagues, the nature of her job requires her to sit in front of a computer screen by herself for long hours.

As someone with a long-time interest in complementary therapies, Jacqui was attracted to training as a Shiatsu practitioner – a very physical and specialized form of massage from Japan. With the encouragement of some friends, and a few work mates, she started the training course that would lead to her qualifying as a practitioner. As her company has a flexi-time arrangement, it was possible for her to rearrange her work hours to accommodate this training.

After three years of hard work, she successfully qualified and wanted to find a way of giving Shiatsu treatments without giving up her software development job. Her employers valued her experience and competence in the job and were keen not to lose her. They agreed to her reducing her hours and she now works three days a week in her original job and spends two days at a complementary health clinic giving Shiatsu treatments.

Someone else who has benefited from an enlightened employer is Haq. His company provides telecoms solutions for other businesses and he has worked there for four years. Haq is also a gifted musician and he and some friends formed a Bangra (Punjabi dance music) group a few years ago and are now building quite a reputation for themselves. The time taken up with rehearsing and performing meant that Haq was finding it difficult to find enough time for the management and administration of the band.

He realized that if he could reduce his working hours to four days a week, he would be able to commit a full day to band management as well as to writing and arranging new songs. With the agreement and support of his employer, Haq is now able to work on fulfilling his musical potential without giving up a job he loves. In return, his employer has cemented Haq's commitment to them and he is now less tired and distracted when he is there.

What is encouraging about both Haq and Jacqui's stories is that they have not had to become fully self-employed to create the kind of flexible and fulfilling working lives they want. Their fulfilment comes from recognizing that they are unlikely to find everything they want in one job. By blending two different professional activities, they have created an overall working life that is satisfying for them.

■ Portfolio working

While Haq and Jacqui have combined two different roles to create their fulfilling working lives, others blend many more. One of the trends in today's way of working is the 'portfolio worker' – someone who derives income from a range of different professional services or skills.

As William Bridges describes in his book, *Jobshift: How to Prosper in a Workplace Without Jobs*, the breakdown of our current concept of the term 'job' reverses a transition seen at the start of the Industrial Revolution. Before 1800, the word 'job' did not refer to one full-time occupation undertaken for a single employer. Rather, it indicated an individual piece of work. In those days, one's work would be made up of a range of different jobs, some of which you did for yourself and some of which you might be paid for. So a craftsman might be engaged in a piece of work for a particular customer and, when that ended, would move on to another job for another customer. But when the grain needed to be harvested, he'd be out in the field helping with that; at other times he'd be tending some livestock he owned. And then there was the maintenance and repair of his tools – not a job he'd be paid for but an essential one nonetheless.

Bridges' book describes how, and why, the landscape of work is changing, with many jobs (in the full-time, employed, sense of the word) disappearing and some people returning to a pre-industrial model of work. This is the model that another writer, Charles Handy, describes as the 'work portfolio'.

In *The Age of Unreason* – written at the close of the 1980s – Handy describes some of the key changes about to take place in the world of business and work. It is interesting to read his book in retrospect (it is still in print, fifteen years on) and see how much of what he predicted has come to pass.

When you see your working life as part of a portfolio of activities, it challenges the notion of seeing work as merely a nine-to-five job. This in turn can liberate you to think more broadly about what work is meaningful for you and how it can be undertaken. My own work is made up of such a portfolio of activities, some of which is paid and some not. Until recently, I used to spend the occasional day serving customers in an independent bookshop. This is what Handy calls *wage work*, where one receives an income for time given. This never accounted for much of my overall income but it was enormously satisfying for me as it fulfilled a long-held ambition.

Most of my income is derived from a range of freelance activities, principally coaching, writing and training. For each of these I am paid a fee on a job by job basis (fee work). Fee work and wage work are the activities from which we earn our income but that doesn't cover all of the work we do. Handy's model describes three kinds of unpaid work. There is *gift work*, such as volunteering or helping out in the community; *home work*, which is all the domestic and family tasks we undertake; and *study work*, which could be taking an evening class, studying for a professional qualification or even reading a personal development book.

What I like about Handy's model is that it encourages us to recognize and value *all* of the work we undertake. Rather than merely considering whatever you do from nine-to-five to be your *work*, thinking about your work portfolio helps you to give attention to all that you are trying to achieve in life. Once you know what is in your portfolio, and which elements are of greatest importance to your fulfilment, you can begin to plan how to make it all fit together. This can be a really helpful way of breaking out of old patterns of thinking about work and beginning to see – like Jacqui and Haq – new opportunities and possibilities. For those who are self-employed, a work portfolio also encourages thinking about how to balance those activities that generate income and those tasks (like marketing, networking and financial management) that support the business but don't directly earn money.

Yet a work portfolio is more than simply a way of thinking about work. It describes the way that many of today's workers are operating. In a return to pre-industrial work patterns, more and more twenty-first century workers do a bit of this and a bit of that. While this is by no means everybody's ideal working life, many of those who work in this way find it enjoyable, fulfilling and rewarding. They get variety in their work as well as independence, flexibility and the opportunity to write their own job description. By taking advantage of the rise in service roles, as well as the need for skilled freelancers and knowledgeable consultants, portfolio workers are making the most of the new culture of work.

■ Taking advantage of current opportunities

There are a number of other contributory factors in the current climate of work that make now a particularly good time to rethink your career. What holds many back from changing career in midlife is their fear and anxiety about the risk they are taking. While the element of risk can never be eliminated, there are a number of factors which mimimize it at the moment, not least the current economic stability.

Unemployment is lower than it has been for thirty-odd years. This offers those who are exploring a new career a safety net if things don't work out. It's not as if you are going to starve. When I wound up a successful training and consultancy business to concentrate on coaching and writing, I was asked by my brother what I'd do if the new business didn't take off. Aside from articulating a fear that I had worked hard to bury deep in the back of my mind, his question was not an unreasonable one. Any good consultant would ask the same thing: what is your contingency plan?

'I'll simply go and get a job in my old line of work,' I heard myself saying. And the relief was immediate. The truth was that I *had* been anxious about taking the risk, for who in their right mind would pull the plug on a going concern to venture into something new? By facing up to the worst-case scenario and thinking it through, I realized that I was never going to be left looking for a dry spot to pitch my cardboard box. Besides, my brother's kids would be going to university soon. They weren't going to be needing their bedrooms any more…

While it might go against the grain for those who remember the unemployment of the 1980s to give up a secure job in orer to try something different, stepping out in a new direction is not the risk it once was. For some people, the worst that could happen is that they end up back in the same type of job they were trying to get away from. Perhaps it really is better to have tried and failed than never to have tried at all.

Yet I can't immediately think of anyone who has had to go back to what they were doing before. For if your career change is thoroughly thought out, well researched and carefully planned, you will probably succeed. Even if you don't end up *exactly* where you were heading when you set off, it is unlikely that you'll ever want to go back. Your new direction will have taken you somewhere more interesting, giving you a taste for the working life you desire.

This might sound glib. After all, you can probably think of someone whose business venture failed, or who has applied 152 times for their dream job and never got an interview. We conjure up these stories to bolster the case for the prosecution that persists inside our heads to justify our fears and anxieties. Those would be the same fears and anxieties that stop us taking action to fulfil our potential, so how helpful are they?

Just because someone took a risk and failed isn't an argument against taking risks. It is an argument for getting it right.

A good job market offers a contingency plan to deal with the worst-case scenario, so instead of focusing too much attention on what might go wrong, put your energy into building on current trends and opportunities that will help you make it work.

■ Fixed-term contracts

One such trend is the rise in short-term or fixed-term contracts. They are often to be found, for example, in the public and voluntary sector, where changes in the way work is funded mean that jobs may only exist for a year or two and when the contract expires so does your ability to pay the rent.

Actually the reality isn't nearly as bleak as it might sound. For those who are interested in making a career change, a fixed-term contract has a lot to offer.

Part of the attraction for some is that many fixed-term jobs are in the public and voluntary sector. One recurring theme I hear is a desire to do something that is of more discernible benefit to others. As one client put it, 'I'm tired of working hard merely to make money for other people. I'd like to do something that directly puts something back into the community.'

There is, of course, an economic argument that wealth generated for others *will* help the community in the long run. Whether or not people share that view isn't really the point here. Rather, it is about how directly they feel their work makes an impact. Workers in all kinds of fields feel less motivated when they don't see the difference their effort makes – a theme we shall return to later on.

Taking a fixed-term contract, then, is one way of moving into a new area of work without making a long-term commitment. If you decide not to stay in that field of work once the contract ends, you can do so without looking as if you're the one who can't make a commitment. Citing 'end of contract' as a reason for leaving will always look better on a CV than 'I hated it and wanted to lock my boss's head in the filing cabinet...'

It is important to note that the end of a fixed-term contract does not always mean the employee is out of a job. Having pointed out the shortcomings of some employers in the previous chapter, it is only fair to recognize the commitment and loyalty of others. It is not necessarily the case that those employers who use short-term contracts are doing so because they are not committed to their staff. Many have no option because they are working within the criteria of funding bodies who operate on, say, three-year funding cycles. While there may be some employers who use fixed-term contracts to paper over the cracks of poor management and planning, there are many good employers who will do all they can to redeploy workers at the end of the contract.

I can think of quite a number of people whose contract has been renewed at the end of the initial period because new funding was received to continue the project. In other cases, employers found (or created) a new position so that the workers could stay within their organization. It is also now the case that employees cannot be kept on short-term contracts indefinitely without the same rights as permanent staff. All in all, fixed-term jobs have a lot to offer those who are exploring a career change and want to test the water first.

■ Changing attitudes to work

Our changing culture of work is only partly attributable to economic stability and the emergence of service opportunities. We have begun to see important changes in social attitudes to work which in turn create new opportunities for those who want to explore a change in career.

Clearly the most significant factor has been improved opportunities for women in the workplace, though only the most naive would suggest that this is anything but a work in progress. Senior management positions are still predominantly in the hands of men, while in the family it continues to be mostly women rather than men who sacrifice career progression in order to have children.

But not universally so. One social attitude to work that is changing is the rise of the househusband – the man who chooses to stay at home and raise the family while the woman develops her career. Although still relatively rare – and sometimes it is an economic decision because the woman is earning more than the man – the choice by some men to focus on homemaking and parenting has several positive impacts.

Not least of these is that it begins to level the playing field, allowing women to be as free to pursue their career as men have been. In spite of the progression towards equality that has been taking place in the workplace, it is still the norm that women will put their career on hold or allow it to plateau in order to raise children. Even when they return to work, it is more likely that their hours will have to fit around family life than the needs of the job.

Where the man chooses to fulfil the homemaking role, the woman finally has the freedom to commit herself to her career to the degree that her male counterparts have long been able. The question is perhaps where she will find such a man, for there is less of a surge than a trickle of willing candidates. Nonetheless, that some men are willing to declare that parenting and domestic work offers them a fulfilling working life begins to open up new possibilities for the women in their lives.

The emergence of the househusband, however, has another intriguing impact. For those who make the choice willingly and freely (rather than economically), they are placing their vocation firmly in the home work section of their portfolio. That is to say, they are declaring that parenting and homemaking is not a second best choice for them but is of itself an innately rewarding and fulfilling career choice. This, rather paradoxically, could help to build the status of homemaking as an acceptable career choice for women.

This point is perhaps best illustrated by the story of Linda, a lifelong administrator who I met when she wanted to identify some alternative career options. Like many people I've met in their early thirties, Linda wanted to do something else for a living but couldn't work out what it would be.

Over the course of several weeks, she explored a range of career options and undertook some exercises to help her recognize what factors contributed to fulfilling work. She also spoke to friends and colleagues who had jobs that appealed to her to find out more about what their work involved. More than many other clients, she really committed herself to the coaching process and to putting in the work needed to rethink her career.

It was only when we were several weeks down the line that Linda revealed her secret dream. I have been surprised by the number of clients who say they don't know what to do for a living, yet secretly nurture a fantasy job that they don't dare articulate – usually because they believe it is unobtainable, risky or that they lack the ability to pursue it. The dream remains a secret because they believe it is too far-fetched, yet in truth such dreams seldom are. Far from wanting to be rock stars, neurosurgeons or astronauts, most fantasy jobs I hear about are entirely realistic but the client lacks the self-confidence or focus to take it seriously. My job is made so much easier when a client reveals their dream as we are usually able to build a plan together for realizing it.

Linda's secret dream was to stay at home and raise a family. 'It's all I've ever really wanted to do,' she told me. 'When I tell my friends about it, I feel they look down on me as if being a full-time mother was a sell-out.' One can understand her friends' perspective on this. If women start aspiring to stay at home and look after the children, it is almost like giving back the hard-fought ground that they have won in the workplace, and at a time when the battle is not yet over.

It is one thing if a woman feels compelled to stay at home because of social conditioning, family pressure or an assumption that she should sacrifice her career to advance that of her partner. If, like Linda, she is under no such pressure but entirely free to choose her vocation and she feels that bringing up the children, looking after the home and being a part of community life is what she wants most, shouldn't that deserve the same status and recognition as a seat at the boardroom table?

Perhaps with men beginning to freely choose home work as their vocation, this will help others to uphold and value the decision of women to do the same rather than seeing it as a sacrifice. Let me stress that I'm not trying to suggest that women need to be rescued from this predicament by men, merely that when those who have never been pressured to stay at home start choosing to do so it affirms that it is perhaps a credible vocational option for some. I also readily admit that many women do not yet have the freedom to choose on this matter and that staying at home *is* their second choice. But where a woman like Linda takes time to examine all of her options and explore her deep-seated motivational needs and satisfiers – and is able to make a truly free choice – if she concludes that a life at home is what she wants to do most, can't we call that her vocation?

Of course, embracing domestic life as a career choice need not be a full-time option. You might be able to do it all. According to Judy Reith, a coach and course leader who specializes in parenting, this is the reality of many people's working lives. 'I haven't encountered a purebred househusband for ages,' she says. 'What is much more common is both parents working reduced hours and sharing the child care which is a great solution for many families.' This is a scenario that encompasses a number of the trends we've looked at – flexibility, portfolio working and a vocational view of parenting.

■ Downshifting

If full-time househusbands are still pretty rare, a more common trend that indicates changing attitudes towards work is downshifting. This is a term that was coined to describe those who make a conscious choice to opt out of the rat race and sacrifice income and consumerism for a better quality of life.

Downshifting really came to the fore in the 1990s on the back of the boom-and-bust years of the previous decade. Before the dole queues had receded to anything like an acceptable level, some people in Britain were getting very, very rich. While many school leavers continued to sign on, others were making the most of the economic boom. This was the era of the yuppie, where bright young things in the city earned bonuses beyond their wildest dreams. Sales of Porsche cars, Rolex watches, riverside apartments and luggage-sized mobile phones shot up. A great deal more money shot up people's noses as cocaine became the *drug de jour*, an eroded septum being the ultimate status symbol for those who had so much money they didn't know what to do with it all.

It didn't last, of course. As Britain collapsed into another recession, the impact on both those who had enjoyed the boom time and those who watched from the sidelines was much the same. It gradually dawned on people that economic stability could not be taken for granted and, by extension, that grounds for an optimistic future were decidedly shaky. In addition many of those who had got rich realized that something was missing. Although they had enjoyed the rewards of their work, it had been a stressful and pressured occupation that had delivered those rewards and one which was not always entirely fulfilling.

Suddenly quality of life became a priority for some people. Having a successful career that delivered a high income and many material benefits was not enough, not if you did not have the time and energy to enjoy them. As the yuppies found partners and began to settle down, work that was in some way meaningful became a greater priority. People started to scale down their lifestyles to take on lower-paid jobs that delivered a better work-life balance. The downshifting trend had started.

Although priorities vary from person to person, certain themes run through the experience of those who downshift. Critically, it is about learning to say 'enough' at the point where lifestyle and ambition seem to be running so far ahead that it is hard to keep up. Downshifters tend to revaluate their relationship with money, not seeing it as an end in itself but something that is required in so far as it facilitates other non-material benefits. They often engage in the community in a new way or put family life higher on the agenda than before. The right house for them is one that meets their needs, not necessarily the biggest one in the street; likewise the car. And time is freed up to focus on developing other aspects of life, including hobbies, talents or socializing.

At the heart of the downshifting trend were workers who chose to seize control of their own life and put what mattered most to them at the centre of it. By breaking out of the cycle of overwork, stress and spiralling consumerism, they took time to reframe their lifestyle on their own terms rather than those of employers, media or peer pressure. It undoubtedly requires courage to downshift and there are many inspirational stories about those who have taken the plunge. We tend to hear less about downshifting than we once did, perhaps because the media has got bored of talking about it. Or perhaps, as I like to think, it is now more common than ever for people to take the initiative and make the right choices for themselves to create a more meaningful life. The downshifters of the 1990s started a trend that not only makes it socially acceptable to drop out of the rat race but proves that it can be a successful and rewarding decision.

By choosing to take advantage of the positive opportunities that exist in today's culture of work, there is no reason why you cannot follow in their footsteps.

■ To think about:

1. What changes in our culture of work have you personally experienced over the years? What opportunities do they offer you in creating a more meaningful working life?

2. What do you *know* that you could sell to employers or clients?

3. Consider what is in your portfolio of work – including both paid and unpaid work. How would you like to change it, or what would need to happen to enable you to commit more time to the work you want to do more of?

4. Whose working life presents an attractive role model for you? What is it that appeals to you about it, and how could you make it your own?

Three: Finding self-expression through work

To define meaningful and fulfilling work for yourself, you may need to unpick the way you have been conditioned to think about your career. A good starting point is to throw away the one question you have probably lived with since childhood: what do you want to be when you grow up?

One reason this is hard to answer at a young age is that it presumes there is a pre-existing job out there with your name on it, one that you will immediately identify with and which in turn will contain all of the key ingredients to deliver a fulfilling and purposeful working life. It is possible to recognize such a job only if:

- You have a clear overview of *all* the options available to you (including understanding what many different job titles mean and appreciating the nature of various professions);
- You understand in detail what a job will feel like before you've even tried doing it;
- You are clear about the various factors that motivate you in your work and are certain that your chosen job will deliver these to you.

These are not issues that most fifteen-year olds have a grasp of when they need to start making important choices that will affect their future occupation.

Those who are able to say from the outset 'I want to be a nurse/ firefighter/engine driver' and hit the nail on the head first time are the lucky ones. For everyone else, the process is rather more complex. And when it comes to careers, potential employers don't generally take a positive view of workers experimenting and testing out options through trial and error. So there is pressure on you to get it right from the outset and commit to it – which is a pity if you later discover that your chosen career is not for you.

The what-do-you-want-to-be question is problematic because it doesn't start with you but requires you to satisfy the needs of the job. Disaffected workers often feel like square pegs in round holes, trying to fit themselves into an assortment of pre-determined jobs that don't quite accommodate them. The conventional approach to finding a career means squeezing yourself into roles that other people have designed. The whole process begins with the job and works backwards to you. The best that many people manage is to aim for the nearest fit based on the information available to them.

Obviously there are good reasons why the world of work needs you to fit a mould that somebody else has designed. But could it be that you've been so busy trying to satisfy the requirements of school and university curricula, and the needs of future employers, that you haven't given sufficient time to gaining an understanding of your own requirements for a meaningful and fulfilling career? In other words, has your career plan been built from the job down rather than from yourself up?

Like many people, you've probably thought about your own needs in terms of pay and conditions, job location, career development opportunities and so on. While these factors are important, they don't define a vocation. They are practical needs that require attention but won't in themselves add meaning to your work.

Finding your own definition of meaningful work requires you to start with yourself and build around you those factors that enhance your sense of purpose and fulfillment. This means describing attractive work in a way that doesn't begin with identifying the right job title or profession but with a list of key criteria that need to be present in a job in order for it to have more meaning for you than merely a path to a pay cheque.

This process is like redecorating and furnishing a well-used room. Here, the room represents your working life. You begin by taking everything out of the room and starting from scratch in thinking about how you will furnish it. Only when you begin with a blank sheet of paper and a mind free of assumptions can you really think creatively and imaginatively about how the room might look its best and meet your needs. But if you presume certain objects must be in the room and have to be worked around, your thinking will always be cramped.

So your starting point is to set aside everything you know and understand about work and how to build a successful career. You are going to put all of this in storage for the time being, as a resource to draw on later. Some of what you remove you will be putting back in later on; that is to say, do not assume you are starting entirely from scratch. Your work experience to date will have taught you a lot about yourself and what is important to you in a job, so as you undertake this review of your working life you'll want to draw on this knowledge to help you pinpoint important criteria. For the time being, though, you should leave nothing in the room that you have to work around. The only thing that should be present is *you*.

■ Personal insight

Everything that ends up in your working life must come from you. Every factor that helps you to understand what gives your work meaning will be an expression of your *Self* because truly vocational work grows out of who you are. It is an external manifestation of your true potential, an outworking of your own personal sense of purpose. While your vocation may not always be easy, you will know you are in the right place when it feels like it's what you were born to do – you almost can't 'not do' it, it is so wrapped up in who you are as a person.

We're not just talking about your skills here but about your passions, values, desires and concerns for others. It is how you see yourself in the world and the role you play within it. It takes, as you might be realizing, a good degree of personal insight about yourself and who you are in order to be able to understand this sense of Self.

Indeed you may have struggled with finding meaningful work largely because you've not yet really explored and understood who you are. If your sense of Self has been defined by how others see you – everything from the role that your family cast you in and your report cards at school, through to guidance from teachers and careers advisers and the jobs you have done – then your view of yourself may be incomplete.

Being able to understand yourself and what makes you tick, being comfortable in your own skin, is a process that takes you to the heart of your personhood. For some, that understanding will come naturally. Perhaps your education and upbringing will have helped you to appreciate this. Or perhaps you've come to know yourself better from the crises in your life. The conflicts, bereavements, break-ups and illnesses that many have encountered will take them closer to knowing their Self more completely.

Many people learn a lot about themselves when they fall in love. The intimacy that a significant relationship brings can also include being presented with some uncomfortable truths about the way you are. Relationships can also cast you into certain roles that may, or may not, be a true expression of you.

Whatever your life experience, you will have encountered some situations where you feel you have grown as an individual – where your sense of self-understanding has been enlarged, or a piece of the puzzle of who you are has fallen into place. Clearly some will have greater insight than others, depending on what life experiences they have had. If you've encountered good counselling or therapy, for example, you may have learned a great deal about yourself. Or if you keep a journal, or have friends that you can be completely open with, you may have gained some self-insight through these routes. But if your life has been uneventful and, like many, you dutifully play your part in whatever role you have been cast by those around you, you may not have taken the time – or seen the need – to reflect on yourself and understand who you really are.

Your insight about your Self grows over the whole of your life. The experiences you encounter and how you deal with them help you to understand more about situations in which you feel comfortable or uncomfortable, thrive or wither. And as far as your vocation is concerned, there are a number of areas of personal insight that you can reflect on that will help you to identify the components of a meaningful working life.

What do you know about your Self?

Taking time to look at yourself, detached from your experience and assumptions about work, may prove to be a daunting experience. It is likely that a key part of your self-image is constructed around the work you do. Your job may be what gives you a sense of Self and of your place in society. Being identified with a particular profession, organization or cause can be a great source of pride and status.

Indeed, losing one's job through redundancy is often a challenging time for those affected because it is not simply the practical problems caused by a loss of income that they have to contend with but the loss of self-esteem and dignity that accompanies it.

This was Ling's experience. Since graduating she had worked for a string of banks within credit control divisions, latterly heading up a department for a major international banking corporation based in the Far East. By the time she was 39, Ling had a rewarding career with a sizeable income, a high degree of confidence in her abilities and a great deal of self-respect which grew out of her profession.

When her bank merged with another, Ling was one of the casualties in the inevitable round of redundancies that followed. In spite of a handsome pay-off and a generous support package – including the services of an outplacement consultant – her redundancy sparked a crisis of confidence. When we spent some time together reviewing her plans for the future, it quickly became clear that Ling was struggling with depression. Just as it seemed she might need the help of a doctor or therapist, she began to talk explicitly about the loss of self-respect and confusion that her redundancy had caused.

What emerged from this conversation was Ling's realization that her view of herself was almost entirely determined by her work, her income and her status at the bank. This created a couple of problems for her over and above the depression she was experiencing. Her search for a new job was undermined by the fact that, now she was out of work, she found it extremely hard to project any kind of self-confidence. Indeed, Ling was avoiding sending out CVs or networking with colleagues because she no longer felt sure of what she had to offer. She had changed from a seemingly confident professional to someone whose career had jumped off the rails.

Yet Ling faced more than a drop in self-confidence. She was struggling to articulate what she wanted to do with her career. Her redundancy exposed a tenuous sense of purpose and direction. She had played the game well, gained the promotions and bonuses that were due to her and built a reputation that helped define her view of herself. Her career was not defined on her own terms but on those of her employer and the culture of the industry she was in. When her job was taken away, it became clear that Ling had little else to hold onto that gave her any sense of Self.

Her breakthrough came – both in finding a new job and banishing her depression – when she realized that she didn't have to depend on her employer to tell her who she was or what her purpose was, and that she could define these for herself. Doing so allowed her to articulate better to prospective employers what her career aims were and to sift out job opportunities that didn't match her own sense of purpose.

Ling's story demonstrates well the difference between letting your Self be defined by external factors such as position and remuneration and rooting yourself in an internal sense of vocation. By working out what meaningful work would entail for her, Ling was able to steady her nerve and seek out a new job that drove her career forward on her own terms and not simply those of her new employer.

■ Self-expression

A major factor that gives your work meaning is when you are able to express your Self through your work. Indeed, disaffected workers often cite not being given space to use their initiative or creativity as a cause of their unhappiness.

The reason these particular factors are commonly mentioned is because using your initiative and creativity are two ways that you manifest your Self in the workplace. That is to say, your work becomes a tangible expression of who you are – your passions, values, interests, character, likes and dislikes, dreams, causes, humour and all the other components that go to make up who you are. When it comes to defining meaningful work, it will help protect you from an experience like Ling's if you are able to take a long hard look at yourself and recognize what factors must be present in your working life for it to be a purposeful expression of yourself.

As we shall see later, meaningful work isn't only about satisfying your own needs. However, one of the indicators that will help you recognize that you are on the right lines is when your work feels as if it pulls together the best bits of who you are. Not just your skills and abilities but all those other attributes that go to make you *you*. Indeed a common remark by those who feel they've found their vocation is that they can't help but do the line of work they are in, so tightly is it bound up with their personality and sense of Self.

In one of Michael Parkinson's many interviews with Billy Connolly, he asked the comedian how he saw himself in the light of his success as a film actor, not to mention his musical career. Connolly replied, without a moment's hesitation, that fundamentally he is a stand-up comedian. In spite of diversifying into different areas of work, stand-up was the real him. It is what he does, almost in spite of himself. You put him in front of people and he will make them laugh.

Steve Westoby is another case in point. A consultant cardiac surgeon for nearly twenty years, he describes surgery as a compulsion. Featured on BBC television's *Your Life in Their Hands*, he said, 'I love doing surgery. If it was a hobby, I couldn't be happier.' It is this sense of absolute simpatico with your work, that tangible expression of your Self, that is the hallmark of meaningful work.

■ Know your values

An excellent starting point is to become clear on what values are important to you in your work. Your values are a core part of the way you operate – key principles that determine the way you behave and function in everyday situations. Sometimes when a person is feeling unhappy or stressed in their work, it is because they are expected to behave in ways, or undertake activities, that are not congruent with their fundamental values.

You can't make your values up; they are a part of you. However, if you are able to name your values, it can help you to understand part of the meaning you seek through your work. You can also have aspirational values – those which you feel are not yet fully present in your work but which you desire to incorporate.

When Jagdish, a 38-year-old accountant at a local authority who wanted to change career, considered ten values that would give his work meaning, he identified the following:

Success	Fun
Empowerment	Justice
Growth and learning	Self-expression
Creativity	Risk-taking
Service	Directness

Identifying these values helped Jagdish to articulate something important about himself and his relationship to his work. By listing his values, he was able to begin considering how his personhood could find expression through his occupation. It is interesting to note that while some of his values are clearly about him being able to enjoy his work (fun, creativity, growth), others relate to the impact that his work has on other people (justice, service, empowerment).

While Jagdish has some business ideas that he would like to explore, his list of values have now helped him to narrow his choices and focus his enquiries on those lines of work that seem most likely to be in keeping with his personal values. If he decides to apply for jobs, he will have a clearer idea of what to ask potential employers about the nature of the job and the culture of the organization.

■ What motivates you?

Another way of understanding your Self in relation to work is to examine what motivates you in the workplace. A simple overview of motivation is provided by the work of Dr David McClelland, who was Professor of Psychology at Boston University until his death in 1998. McClelland's work focused on human behaviour and motivation in the workplace and he developed a model of motivational needs that breaks them down into three categories:

- Need to *achieve* (such as solving problems, meeting targets, mastering a skill, improving something, increasing efficiency)
- Need to *affiliate* (such as gaining a sense of belonging, building good relationships, being identified with a group or organization)
- Need to *influence* (such as being able to affect outcomes, overseeing others, gaining power, having responsibility)

McClelland believed that each individual's motivation was powered by these three needs but that the balance of needs would vary from person to person. While some people may be motivated by a fairly even spread between them, others will be driven by one (or perhaps two) more than the other(s).

While there are tests you can take to measure your degree of motivation in each of these three categories, I have found that most people who have encountered the model on management workshops are instinctively able to understand where they fit on it. Achievement, affiliation and influence provide a good shorthand way of understanding the different ways in which people are driven at work.

Which of these needs does your instinct tell you motivates you most in your work?

Someone that you might describe as a 'people person' is often driven by a need to affiliate. Some of the colleagues and clients I've met who work in the caring professions or in some aspect of social service or voluntary work would be motivated in this way. People in technical, campaigning or sales jobs will often identify most with achievement, while those in management, politics or training might be driven by a need to influence. These are only general illustrative examples and it is important to stress that people in these professions may be motivated principally by needs other than those I've just cited. In any case, all of us are motivated by all three needs to some degree – it is merely a question of the extent to which one need might be more dominant.

McClelland's thinking about motivation is one example of a model which can help to simplify a complex subject and there are many other examples of research and thinking which offer shorthand ways of understanding your Self in relation to work.

■ Personality profiles

For example, a recent study suggests that we are born with certain traits that influence our choice of career. According to Mark Lythgoe of the Institute of Child Health, artists and scientists exhibit markedly different traits, with scientists more inclined towards systemizing while artists show a greater tendency towards more empathic qualities.

'Systemizing traits,' said Lythgoe, 'is the drive to understand a system from inputs and outputs – whether that's a motor system (your car at the weekend), a sociological, a geological, a cultural system; or whether it's just a single cell from its inputs and outputs.'

The empathic traits of artists, on the other hand, include communication and language skills as well as an ability to identify with the feelings of others. The study, which Lythgoe collaborated on, was cross-referenced with two other pieces of research that measured the levels of pre-natal testosterone present in the womb. Babies with lower levels of pre-natal testosterone showed more empathic qualities while those with increased levels had 'increased ability for mental rotation tasks (sort of visual-spatial tasks) which is part of being a systemiser.'

Lythgoe concludes that, although career choice is not pre-determined, 'we perhaps have a predisposition via these traits to take on board information that lead us to certain occupations later on.'

While the world of work obviously doesn't fall neatly into artists and scientists, you can probably think of people you know – perhaps even yourself – who clearly demonstrate the traits of either systemizers or empathizers. Identifying with such 'types' is another way that you can gather some clues about yourself and how you relate to your work. There is certainly no shortage of models available – Myers-Briggs, Belben, Learning Styles, and the Enneagram are just a few of those that categorize various personality types in ways that help to explain what drives and distinguishes you.

What I like about these models is they never say one personality type is better than another – all have their strengths and drawbacks and they can provide a helpful way of simplifying how you see aspects of yourself at work. In particular, they can help you to gain clarity on your preferred style of working – the way you naturally like to operate, function and communicate in the workplace.

I'm not so keen when 'types' are imposed on people by employers without each individual being given the opportunity to engage with the model and discuss where they agree and disagree with its analysis of them. No model or type is 100 per cent accurate in describing you, and such profiles are of most use when you are given the opportunity to reflect and consider how much you identify with their description of you.

While such models won't tell you what career you should be in, they will help you to understand how your character and personality affect the kind of work you enjoy and the way you approach it. For many people this is an illuminating process that can contribute to improving their working life and thinking about how they move it forward.

If you'd like to try some profiling tests online, there are some websites listed at the back of the book.

■ Contribution

Although much of what we've been talking about until now relates to your Self, there is one vital aspect to motivation that significantly adds meaning to work – the impact your work has on others.

Everybody likes to feel their work makes a difference and it is a necessary component of meaningful work that the results of your efforts make a difference. This is sometimes referred to as *service* – not altogether a bad way of expressing this concept. In those careers that are traditionally viewed as vocational, such as medicine, education, or religion, it is easy to understand what service might mean. But what if you work in telecommunications or civil engineering, as an administrator or a bus driver?

In fact, most jobs have a service element to them. We are usually in work because we are helping to solve a problem or meet a need for somebody else. Sometimes workers lose touch with this aspect of their work, perhaps because they are quite far removed from the end result. Regrettably others have lost any concept of service because they just don't care, perhaps because their employer is exploiting them or because they have become too absorbed in their own interests and rights. In either case a loss of any sense of service undermines both personal fulfilment and professional conduct. The poor state of customer service offered by many companies in Britain today is a direct result of them taking their eye off the needs of the customer and concentrating on the bottom line of their balance sheets.

I realize that the word *service* may be suggestive of a kind of self-sacrificial giving for the needs of others. In some cases, of course, that is exactly the sort of service that people might provide. But the notion of service is bigger than that. For this reason, I prefer to talk about *contribution*. In other words, in what way do you want your work to make a difference and by whom or what will that impact be experienced?

This is really a way of engaging with some kind of wider vision about the nature of your work over and above your own personal fulfilment. Such a vision helps to explain the purpose that one's work has and the outcome it will lead to. Your vision can be grand in scale or specific in its scope, regardless of the status, income level and title of the job being done. The person who collects the recycling from outside your house could be a passionate environmentalist; a domestic cleaner could be on a mission to enable parents to spend more time with the family; the sales person in a mobile phone shop in the high street could be excited by helping people to communicate more easily.

These might seem fanciful notions but if your work does not connect to any wider sense of purpose, then it is going to be hard for it to move beyond being just a job. And from there it is a short step towards feeling uninspired or cynical. For those who currently feel disaffected by their work, it may be the realization that the contribution their work makes does not interest or excite that spurs them into rethinking their career. In looking for an alternative, gaining a clear idea of the kind of difference you want to make is a valuable step in identifying new options. You don't need to know what kind of profession or job you're looking for to be able to describe the contribution you want to make. You can do this in general terms, then add your definition to the landscape of your working life as another key criterion to satisfy in order for your work to have meaning.

For example, Arthur wants to give up his work as a sales manager for an electronics company. He's not yet decided what to do instead but knows that he wants his work to tap into his passion for healthy living. After years of a sedentary desk job, his weight ballooned to 17 stone on a diet of burgers, ready meals and chocolate bars. His wife bought him a session with a personal trainer as a birthday gift one year, hoping he'd take the hint. He did and, through a combination of prolonged exercise and switching to a diet of wholefoods, he lost five stone in weight and rediscovered levels of energy and well-being that he'd never previously experienced. He now coaches a young people's football team in his spare time and is studying a course in nutrition.

Arthur's experience has given him an evangelical zeal to help others to discover the benefits of healthier living for themselves. At this stage he has yet to decide what specific form his new career will take but he knows the contribution he wants to make in enabling others to feel fitter, more confident and energized so that they can get more out of life.

Rebecca, on the other hand, does not share Arthur's sense of being on a big mission. However, she is no less clear about the importance of the element of service to her work. She is a project manager for a firm of IT consultants and is responsible for co-ordinating support and communication with staff out on the road. She knows that her job enables the consultants to be in the right place at the right time, properly briefed about the clients they are visiting and equipped with the right resources for the job. Rebecca is not especially fired up about IT *per se* but she enjoys the job, feels it makes the most of her skills and has great rapport with her colleagues. For her, the difference she makes is that she enables them to do their job swiftly, efficiently and to the high standards for which her firm has a reputation. By keeping her focus on the contribution she makes, Rebecca stays motivated and fulfilled and finds meaning in a job for a firm whose essential business she has had to learn to appreciate.

Finding meaning in your work by establishing the difference you make can just as easily be accomplished in the intrinsic sense of service of Rebecca as in the lofty ideals of Arthur. It doesn't matter whether your mission is to change the world or to service your colleagues well, just as long as you have a mission of some sort that resonates with you.

■ Creativity

So far we've explored the need to understand your Self in order to better express it through your work. While self-expression means bringing more of your Self to the work you do – that is, being free to *be* yourself in the workplace and having the capacity to make your work an extension of your personhood – the opportunity to undertake specifically creative tasks is one of the most common ways that people seek self-expression.

When I talk about creativity, I don't simply mean being 'arty', although it could include that. People are creative in all sorts of ways in their work, from solving problems and working out better ways of doing a task or project to generating ideas and designing innovative products and services. When people say, 'I'm not creative,' it simply isn't true. Everyone is creative, but the form of their creativity and the skills they can use in exercising it will be different from the next person.

When staff are deprived of this kind of creative outlet, a drop in motivation won't be far behind. If a workplace is so dependent on systems and procedures that workers have little or no scope to devise solutions to problems, or exercise their own initiative, then an important source of self-expression is being closed off.

Creativity, and creative thinking, is something that can be nurtured. One company that tries to foster this in their staff is Ernst & Young.

They have built a strong relationship with the visual arts over the last ten years and their sponsorship of major art exhibitions provides a springboard for a range of initiatives that encourages staff to nurture their creative thinking. This might involve attending exhibition talks given by curators, engaging in projects with artists to learn how they think about their work, coaching schoolchildren in photography or volunteering on arts projects with homeless people. So how does an encounter with the visual arts help nurture creativity in staff that work for one of the largest firms of professional advisers specializing in auditing, tax and corporate finance? Are they suddenly getting colourful with their spreadsheets?

Not according to Nicky Martin, Ernst & Young's Head of Marketing for the Arts. 'We want people to think creatively and differently, but in the right context. We're putting people in a new environment to do something different and then bring what they've learned from that experience back into the workplace. Our staff tend to think quite logically because that's the nature of the business plus they have to conform to many set systems and procedures because we're subject to financial regulation. Projects which give them a certain kind of creative experience can encourage things like quick thinking, teamwork, presentation skills or devising innovative solutions to business problems, because they've learned to see and do things in a different way.'

Ernst & Young's projects with the visual arts interested me for a number of reasons. They are deploying a well-established strategy for encouraging creative thinking by offering staff the opportunity to experience something new. Writers and consultants who specialize in creativity at work have long encouraged people to expose themselves to the kind of music, art, literature or performance that they wouldn't normally encounter as a way of kick-starting the brain into breaking out of established patterns of thinking. Indeed, simply putting yourself in a situation where you experience the creativity of others – regardless of whether you like it or not – can really boost your ability to generate ideas or solve problems.

I also like the way that Ernst & Young recognize that creativity isn't just about art. Although the visual arts happen to be the medium they use to nurture creativity, the creative thinking and output that they require relates to how people do their job – everything from how they might organize their work, give a presentation or collaborate with colleagues, through to innovation and problem-solving. It goes to show that there is potential for people to be creative in many different spheres and professions and not merely those we usually associate with the word *creative*. For Ernst & Young, both the business and the employees benefit because fostering creativity in staff can help to release their potential and build performance, while giving individuals room for self-expression in their work builds satisfaction.

In identifying meaningful work for yourself, it is helpful to try to establish what kind of creativity is important to you. It may be that you have a particular skill or flair that you want to utilize in your work or it may be that you want the creative freedom to make decisions, solve problems or be innovative. Take time to consider what kind of work environment would bring out the creative side in you and what particular forms of creativity you want to express through your work.

■ Wholeness

Although there are other more specific factors that contribute to meaningful work, such as utilizing your skills and attributes, I've started with understanding your Self because it is necessary to have this degree of insight in order to construct a meaningful career around oneself. One of the reasons that people are hitting the buffers over their career when they reach their thirties and forties is because by then they've begun to accumulate enough life experience and self-understanding to realize why they are mismatched to the job they are in. It is much harder (though not always a problem) for 15-year-olds to know enough about themselves to make choices about their career that fit who they are.

It is human nature to be on a constant quest for wholeness or completion. Some people are very focused and clear about what this means for them; others live with a vague nagging feeling that not all is well but they can't put their finger on what the problem is. For some, their quest for wholeness will be expressed through their faith, partner or children. While not seeking to diminish these aspects of life, I believe that work is the other key component in delivering wholeness in that it provides a significant way of fulfilling your potential. For that to take place a degree of self-knowledge is required that your life and work to date may or may not have given you.

As you begin to define the landscape of a meaningful working life, put yourself at the focal point of the picture and take time to determine the essential criteria that will allow you both to express yourself and fulfil your potential. Doing so will enable you to move forward in your journey towards wholeness.

■ To think about...

We've explored some key components of meaningful work that relate to self-expression, which in turn can help you to landscape a meaningful working life. In particular, take time to reflect on:

1. What would be on your list of values in order for your work to be an expression of your Self?
2. What motivational needs must be satisfied through your work?
3. What do you know about your own personality and your preferred working styles?
4. What difference do you want your work to make? Formulate a Statement of Purpose that describes the impact you'd like to have. You don't yet need to know what job or profession you desire in order to do this exercise – indeed it often works best if you break away from thinking about careers in terms of job titles or professions and think more openly and creatively about the work you want to do.
5. What kind of creativity do you need to be able to express through your work?

Four: Auditing your skills and abilities

A key asset that you bring to your working life is the set of skills that you are able to offer to employers or clients. It is a reminder of the stark reality that work can't simply focus on satisfying your own needs but must offer something that is desired by others.

This is all part of the finely tuned balance that contributes to meaningful work. Given that it would be foolish to throw yourself rashly into work you enjoy but for which nobody will hire you, it is rather more likely that you've focused on the other side of this balance – gaining and demonstrating the kinds of skills, experience and qualifications that you understand will smooth the path to a successful career.

Setting aside the question of who defines 'success' in this scenario, the trap that many of today's workers have fallen into is that the skills they are able to present to employers have been studiously gained at the employer's behest and don't necessarily portray an accurate or rounded picture of their overall abilities. Indeed, a common source of frustration for workers is the feeling that they have skills that are not being recognized or utilized in their jobs.

Work is fulfilling when it makes the most of the skills and abilities at your disposal, not just the qualifications and hands-on experience that you've accumulated over the years but also your natural talents and qualities. It could be that some formal training you have undertaken has helped to develop a natural talent. This is the best-case scenario. Steve Redgrave, one of Britain's greatest Olympic champions, had his rowing talent spotted and nurtured by a teacher at school, enabling him to continue training to develop his potential. A good school will do this – spot talent in pupils and cultivate it, whether in academic or extra-curricular fields, encouraging them to push forward to make the most of it once they leave school.

Yet there is a limit to the opportunities that schools can provide to spotlight talent. Your potential might never have been noticed simply because your particular niche wasn't on the curriculum. And even if it was, that is no guarantee that you would have been encouraged to take it seriously. When today's generation of thirty- and forty-somethings were at school, science and technology subjects were highly valued. If you showed a talent for, say, maths, physics or technical studies, then you fitted the education system's assumption that those were the skills needed by British industry (which promptly imploded just as you left school or college). If your flair was in art, music, sport or drama, it was highly likely that you would be advised to go out and get a proper job, putting your talent on the back-burner as at best a hobby.

So talent spotting is a game that is fraught with difficulty. Many workers concentrate on playing the system by finding out what job opportunities are available and then gaining the right qualifications to get employed. For many people it is simply enough to get a secure job with good prospects, never mind one that will make full use of their abilities and potential *and* deliver a fulfilling vocation.

If this echoes your experience, then it is possible that you've never audited your skills in a comprehensive way but, rather, have learned to see yourself as others want to see you. Perhaps you've become defined by the career you're in rather than by who you are. Po Bronson, in his fascinating collection of case studies of people who have made mid-life career changes (entitled *What Should I Do with My Life?*) writes about what he calls 'the Inevitable Cocktail Party Question' where our shorthand method of introducing ourselves to one another is in response to '… and what do you do?'

It's a great question to answer if what you 'do' is an expression of who you are, but for many it is an uncomfortable enquiry because it reinforces the gap that exists between Self and job. It can be a potent reminder that you've learned to define yourself in ways by which others want to measure you because you have moulded yourself to fit the expectations of family, teachers and employers. Perhaps you were the technical one in your family? Or the dreamy one? Or the arty one? The roles that we begin to take on can soon become constricting if they only serve to satisfy other people's expectations of you. Rather than learning to discover yourself and your talents to the full, you merely end up conforming.

That becomes a problem if you lose sight of how important it is to fulfil your potential. Meaningful work requires that you make full use of both your natural and learned abilities. In this way you bring the best of yourself to your work because it engages all areas of your talents, aptitude and qualities.

So in assessing the skills that you might bring to your vocation you won't only look at those you've learned along the way but also at those you've always had, those you take for granted and those you have an inkling you might have. The goal here is to audit your skills set as fully as possible with a view to planning how you can utilize it as comprehensively as possible in the work you do.

■ Learned skills

We'll start with those skills you have made an effort to learn because these are probably the abilities that you are most likely to be able to quote readily. For example, these are the skills that you are likely to mention on your CV because you have acquired them via your work experience as well as through your qualifications and training.

In assessing your learned skills, you might want to distinguish between those you value and those you don't. That is to say, you may have learned to do some things that were a necessity at the time but which don't figure in your notion of meaningful work. For example, I have learned how to use a spreadsheet (just). It doesn't mean I'm proud of the fact or that I wouldn't jettison having to do a tax return every year given half the chance. So, in listing your skills, you might want to set apart those that don't really resonate with your sense of vocation but are nonetheless part of the skills set you've acquired.

Another way of thinking about learned skills is to single out those that you feel have helped you to develop or nurture a raw talent you already had. Take, for example, Lucille: she has always had good organizational abilities and, as a child, played libraries and shops, setting up little systems for stocktaking and checking books out of her 'library'. As a teenager she got involved in organizing clubs and events at school and church. She trained and got a job as an administrator in a firm where a manager spotted her ability at project management. She championed Lucille's development within the organization and encouraged her to take on this new role, backed up by appropriate training and a qualification. Lucille's development into project management is a good example of where a learned skill built on an existing natural ability and developed it further.

Any aspect of your training or work experience that develops a talent you already had is particularly significant because it capitalizes on your potential. There is often a close link between work that comes naturally and work that you enjoy doing. Adding value to a natural ability by developing it further through training or experience stands you a much greater chance of finding meaning in your work.

■ Natural skills

It is tempting to value only those skills that you've worked hard to acquire. After all the effort you went through to develop that ability or gain that qualification, you are not easily going to forget that it is part of the set of skills you are able to bring to your career. Such skills are also likely to be those that employers are seeking and, because they value them, you will be more conscious of their worth. You might also have learned to do something you love, valuing it because of the enjoyment it brings you.

For all these reasons it is easy to overlook other natural abilities that you are able to bring to your work. Like Lucille, you may have a gift for organization. You might be a natural communicator, or a leader. Some people have a very technical frame of mind and are naturally curious about how things work. Others have a natural eye for design or colour or have a flair for cooking or for making things with their hands. The list is endless. Just because you have not had to work hard at something doesn't mean it is not important to you. If you are to realize your whole potential, natural abilities must find an outlet somewhere – if not through work, then certainly in some other aspect of life.

When gifted people are advised to 'get a proper job' rather than develop such talents, they are not being helped. Such advice, though usually well meaning, is often the product of a parent or teacher's own insecurity about financial stability or 'success'. While that is not unreasonable grounds for the advice, the irony is that your greatest chance of success is to fulfil your potential by making the most of talents you have.

There can be a tendency to undervalue natural ability simply because it comes easily; using it is possibly even fun. The dregs of the Protestant work ethic that swill about in society certainly don't encourage you to pursue work that is fun or easy. Work should be hard, involving discipline, effort and long hours – shouldn't it?

Actually, those who pursue their vocation often *do* work long hours and may need to be disciplined to get things done. But to work hard because you enjoy it is rather different from pushing yourself and striving because you are forced to.

It might be the case that your natural skills will still benefit from some training. Raw talent sometimes has to be refined before you can really capitalize on it and turn it into a vocation. This is the best kind of training to undertake because you do it for what it will teach you. I encounter many people who think about training purely in terms of the qualification it will give them and the doors that will open to them as a result. But they are not especially interested in the content of the training *per se*. When a course helps to develop your abilities, there is a much stronger chance that the learning itself will be stimulating, rewarding and enjoyable.

My work ethic says that satisfaction and meaning will only come through using the abilities you have been given and that failing to utilize your natural skills is both dishonouring to yourself and likely to leave you feeling unfulfilled.

There are some natural talents that, even when developed through training, are still perceived as high risk. Music, art and drama, for example, are areas where you may know someone who has struggled to make a success of themselves. Often those who observe others in this situation are measuring their success by their own standards, rather than those of the person who is pursuing their potential, for instance the parent who measures their daughter's success in terms of the house she lives in or the friend who thinks his mate has failed because he can't afford to dine out at the best restaurants.

It is important to recognize that vocational work is sometimes successful on its own terms rather than those imposed by friends and family who are not themselves a part of that field of work.

I think part of the trap that people fall into when thinking about talents in areas such as sport, art, music and drama is that they bring to them preconceived ideas about how these talents will be expressed. It is not the case that, say, a person with a musical ear will automatically want to be a performer – or indeed will be suited to performing. Musicians also conduct, teach, produce, engineer and compose. What matters is that the musical person finds a channel for that talent.

So in stocktaking your skills, it is necessary to recognize the natural abilities that you can bring to your working life and to value them on their own terms rather than dismiss them.

■ Skills you take for granted

It is often easier to recognize skills in other people than to acknowledge your own in full, particularly if you are aware of something they can do that you cannot. If you've had a particular ability all your life, or have learned to do something well over the course of a fifteen- or twenty-year career, it may be harder to appreciate what you have.

I have had many conversations with people who, when listing their skills, completely overlook a whole range of competences that they take for granted. It's as if they assume that anybody can do such-and-such and it is therefore not worth mentioning. Computer literacy is a case in point. Now that so many of us have to use a PC in our work (not to mention the one we have at home), it is easy to forget how much we've learned to adapt and incorporate IT skills into our working lives. When I ask clients about their skills set, surprisingly few remember to mention their ability to use a computer. And yet there are many people out there who don't have this skill. Depending on your line of work, the types of task you undertake on a computer and the sorts of programmes you use will vary.

An effective audit of your skills set will include everything you are able to do, whether or not you value all those skills. The problem is that you may take certain skills for granted to such an extent that you can't even identify them. Often it will take a friend, relative or colleague to help you recognize everything you have to offer. If others are better able to see your skills than you, then you may have to ask them. While it might offend your modesty to go begging compliments from others, it is sometimes a necessary step in assessing yourself. Besides, a good friend or supportive colleague will often be happy to help you with this, particularly when they understand it is part of a career review.

When Sheila, a reserved and quietly spoken administrator, agreed to list her skills and abilities, she balked at the idea of asking others for feedback. Nonetheless, as she was serious about rethinking her working life, she gritted her teeth and got on with it. She discovered that colleagues valued her eye for detail. Not only did they often give her written work to proofread but they also included her in discussions about projects because she was the one who could step back from an activity and see its wider and far-reaching implications. While Sheila had assumed this was simply part of her job as an administrator (or 'just an administrator' as she self-deprecatingly put it), she learned that she had an important role within her department based on a particular knack that she was uniquely able to offer. From her perspective, she just did what she did. It had never occurred to her that when she spotted oversights in project plans, or picked up on others' spelling mistakes and typos, she was bringing to her work a skill that others wished they had.

This was an important lesson for Sheila for another reason, too. She had always put herself down in terms of what she could offer. She felt her skills were bland and unexciting. She couldn't play the piano like her friend, Adam, or generate amusing and clever slogans like her colleague Steve. She wasn't an accountant or an architect or a teacher. She was 'just an administrator who does all the usual stuff that administrators do'.

Sheila's skills audit began to help her see herself as Sheila. Certainly, a part of her skills set was shared by others but, as she began to think seriously about what she had to offer, she began to understand where her strengths lay and that she embodied a unique and particular combination of abilities that made her her. She also learned to value parts of her character that she had underrated in herself; her introspective nature, she realized, allowed her to take a back seat in meetings and let everyone else do the talking until she spotted the point that the noisy ones had overlooked because they had been so engaged in the politics of discussion.

■ Desired skills

As well as taking stock of the skills and abilities you already possess, it is worth setting aside time to consider those skills you would like to develop or learn. Is there something you think you'd be good at if you were given the chance to learn? Like the character Billy Elliot, in the film of the same name, do you watch what others are doing and think to yourself 'I'd like a go at that?'

One of the reasons I think *Billy Elliot* was such a successful movie is that it resonated with many people's desire to do something different or new for which a courageous step would be required. Billy followed his instincts by trying something despite little encouragement from those around him. Ballet wasn't for boys in a mining community.

Do you have an inkling about something you think you'd be good at? What's holding you back?

A friend of mine started learning to play the saxophone in his late thirties when his son began taking lessons at school. He's got his own instrument now and has performed together with some colleagues. He could have told himself he was too old to learn to play an instrument. He could have worried about failing, or the cost of buying an instrument. Or, or, or...

Instead he just got on with it, took some lessons and practised for half an hour every evening. You'll probably never see him playing at Ronnie Scott's but nonetheless he's pursued a long-cherished ambition that has given him both satisfaction and opportunity.

Whether the skills you want to develop are for work or play, the key to following your desires is about being yourself. People's dreams become unrealistic when they are trying to be somebody else or aspire to a level that is genuinely beyond their ability. But if your development stems from an extension of your Self, your abilities and your experiences, real growth and success are eminently achievable.

Ian Fleming, the writer who created James Bond, lived all his life in the shadow of a brilliant older brother who was critically acclaimed for his literary output. Fleming's Bond novels, on the other hand, which he didn't start writing until he was in his forties, were openly ridiculed within his social circle. While always conscious of his brother's greater success, Fleming's success in creating one of fiction and cinema's lasting icons arose from his reflecting both his own character and his wartime experiences in his writing. Rather than fruitlessly trying to emulate his brother's success, he developed his own writing style in another genre and made it his own. Fleming's Bond novels may not be great literature but they are characteristically *his* and still in print today.

Where you have an inkling about something you would be good at, and which you feel would help you to realize your potential, give it a go. Find out about courses in your area. Talk to friends or acquaintances who can already do what you want to learn. Do some related voluntary work. Hire a tutor and get some lessons. Test your inkling out. You won't discover what possibilities are open to you unless you take some action and there is no failure in trying something out. The real failure is never to have tried at all.

■ Stretch yourself

It is often the case that moments of real growth occur at times when you have to extend yourself outside the normal limits of your confidence. Putting yourself in a new situation, or trying your hand at something that is unfamiliar, can be a scary business. You can perhaps recall a time, such as learning to drive or speaking in public for the first time, where your anxiety levels were such that you'd rather have walked away. But by sticking with it you were able to learn and acknowledge new levels of ability in yourself. Working life is often full of these scary moments, yet many people will testify to the way that their career was able to move forward because of the personal development that these opportunities provided.

Being prepared to stretch yourself is often a part of vocational work. Whether that involves finding the courage to make a bold career move or simply saying 'yes' to new opportunities that arise within your current job, it is likely that key moments that help to create meaning in your work will arise from your willingness to push yourself forward. This means that there will be a constant learning process under way throughout your professional life. As you audit your skills set – learned, natural, undervalued or desired – you may find it helpful to consider how you keep extending and developing your abilities. This could involve learning new skills, taking existing ones into a new situation or continuing to hone those you already possess.

It is sometimes useful to look back over your career history and track the growth and development of the skills at your disposal. When were the key learning moments? What helped you to develop and grow in your work? How did you make choices about which skills to develop or what opportunities arose that enabled this to happen naturally? It is likely that some of your skills were attained through formal training but it would perhaps be interesting to identify any informal circumstances and events that allowed you to develop work skills.

Reflecting on your professional development in this way may offer some useful clues about how you can create the circumstances in which to grow in the ways you want. And if you are able to recognize that certain moments of real growth occurred at times when you had to extend yourself, hopefully it will encourage you to seek opportunities where you have to step outside your current comfort zone.

■ Vocational skills versus hobby skills

In doing a skills audit, you may find you have to make a judgment about whether a skill you possess or desire has the potential to be a part of your career or whether it is only ever going to be a 'spare time' pursuit. This is a complicated question, one that is much easier to work through with individuals on a one-to-one basis.

It hinges on a couple of factors: are you able to exercise all of your skills and abilities within your working life, or is something left over? How well are you able to balance realism with a willingness to accept your capacity for greater things?

For example, how do you decide if your great singing voice holds the potential to turn you into the next Britney/Usher or Kiri/Placido? Should you really push yourself to explore your potential as a singer? Or instead focus on your career as an accountant and join the local choir?

The answer may rest on factors such as:

1. Are you better at singing or accountancy?
You could evaluate your competence and potential in both fields. In assessing the skills that you can bring to your work, what are your relative strengths in terms of how well you can exercise one skill against another? And if you were to commit to developing yourself in one of these skills, which one are you most likely to shine at? These are questions that are tough to answer by yourself, so you would perhaps need to get the insight and assessment of experts in the respective fields.

2. How much do you want to be a singer?
Your decision about where to focus your effort will also need to take account of your depth of passion for both accountancy and singing. Which career would give you the greatest sense of fulfilment and engagement? If your job as an accountant is dissatisfying, is that because it's not really your vocation or is it because you've yet to find the right context in which to exercise it? Or is singing the one thing you've dreamt about for years, the secret fantasy that you have nursed because you feel it really is your vocation?

3. How well are you able to commit to making it happen?

If you choose the singing option, you will probably have to overcome a great deal of discouragement, both from inside your own head and from those around you. Well-meaning friends will suggest you are mad to give up a solid career in accountancy to pursue something as insecure and unpredictable as singing. Their comments will probably resonate with your own internal insecurities. But that doesn't mean that accountancy is really your calling – only that fear of failure and instability might be pushing you away from what you really want to do. Tough call, huh?

Your decision is going to rest on a complex matrix: realistically assessing your skills, your own determination to follow your career of choice and a clear judgment on your part about which talent is most likely to lead to an external expression of your Self.

For many people, the choice won't be as stark as singing versus accounting. You might find a way of blending most of your key skills into your working life. You might find that some get left behind but it won't matter because you are rewarded by the work you are doing. Or you might decide that setting aside a particular talent or interest to pursue as a hobby will provide the perfect counterbalance to help you rest and recuperate during time away from your vocational work.

■ Holistic work

Underlying everything you do when auditing your skills is the premise that your fulfilment in a career will come when you can bring all of yourself to the work that you do. As you evaluate the different abilities that you possess, and those you want to develop, you can use this information to consider new opportunities and directions in which to take your working life. In this way, doing what comes easily is just as valuable as those talents you have striven to learn. Those skills you have a passion for or a yen to try out have as much to teach you about meaningful work as those which others have made you learn. As such, your future skill development is likely to be a mixture of these elements: the natural *you* blended with the *you* that work experience and training helped to create. In fulfilling your potential, you can only make the most of yourself when you know what you have to offer. That has as much to do with the skills you want to go ahead and test out in the future as those you have already demonstrated in your career history.

■ To think about...

We've looked at how you can acquire an accurate snapshot of the skills, abilities and talents that you can bring to working life. Now:

1. List the skills you have acquired through training and work experience. Which do you want to carry forward into a vocational career, and which could you happily leave behind? Are there any skills you've been trained in which you feel have helped you to refine raw talent?

2. Look at your natural skills and abilities. What were you born with that you can do well? What have you have a natural flair for? What friends or colleagues could you ask to help you identify skills that you may not recognize or value in yourself?

3. What skills would you like to acquire? Do you have any notion or inkling about something you would be good at if you had the opportunity? What steps could you take to explore this further?

4. How do you rank your skills and abilities in terms of competence and potential? Which ones really strike a chord with your sense of Self? And with which are you going to have the greatest chance of succeeding in creating meaningful work for yourself?

Five: The right work environment

Even the most rewarding jobs can be ruined by the setting in which you are expected to work. Poor policy decisions, lack of clear management, inadequate resources, difficult relationships with colleagues or unappealing working conditions are just some of the factors that undermine people's motivation in the workplace.

From the many accounts I've listened to, it is clear that a lot of today's workers struggle to balance the positive aspects of their work with the frustrations of the environment in which they are expected to operate. We've all heard about the difficulties some teachers have with pupil discipline; or the long hours that junior doctors have to work; or the bureaucracy that keeps police officers off the beat and in the station.

So far we've looked at what, for you, is the key component in your environment – yourself. Yet in order to truly thrive in your work and be able to give the best of yourself, other aspects of your environment must be such that they support rather than hinder your efforts.

Even if you are still figuring out an alternative career, you can still reflect on your work experience to date and consider what you already know about the kind of environment that brings out the best in you. And if you feel you're in the right job but can't quite put your finger on why you don't feel as motivated as you'd like, I hope this chapter will bring into focus some key issues in the landscape that surrounds you.

■ Personal effectiveness

Your work environment should support you in performing to the peak of your ability – if there is anything (or anyone) around you that gets in the way of your personal effectiveness, it is inevitable that you will feel frustrated. To fulfil your potential, you will need to be clear on what you require to help you work *the way you work best*.

This means taking your needs seriously, in itself something that can be a challenge. Many people resign themselves to putting up with the frustrations of a difficult workplace, culture or management style. After all, other people are coping with it so why shouldn't you? When certain frustrations are the norm within your organization or profession, it is easy to assume the problem lies with you, not them. So the reality for many workers is that they tolerate a difficult work environment, setting their own needs to one side.

What makes a work environment 'difficult'? It may be that there are genuine problems in the way the work is set up, resourced or managed. There is certainly no shortage of thoughtless or mean-spirited bosses in the world, so environmental frustrations can certainly stem from that. But a difficult work environment can also exist within excellent companies. Every organization has its own culture, mindset, values and ways of operating. A competitive work environment, for example, will enable some people to thrive because that is what brings out the best in them – for others it will undermine their ability to do their best. That an employee might struggle within that environment doesn't mean the workplace is inherently bad, merely that it is wrong for them.

So getting the right *fit* between jobs and workers is not just a question of whether they have the right skills and experience for the work. It is also a matter of understanding what kind of environment brings out the best in the individual. In making the most of your own working life, being clear on the kind of environment that helps you to shine will be an important component.

While your personal effectiveness can be hindered by environmental factors, it is not the setting of your work that makes you good at what you do or gives you satisfaction. A positive work environment will streamline your ability to do your best by removing obstacles that slow you down or get in your way but in itself it does not add meaning. This is an important point to recognize before you begin to identify your environmental needs as it is easy to get caught up in material factors that have little to do with enabling you to follow your vocation. Like petulant rock stars who won't perform unless certain flavours of sweeties are available in their dressing room, it's easy to confuse perks with genuine needs. So before you start compiling your own workplace riders, bear in mind that your environmental needs are what will help you perform to the best of your ability.

■ People in your environment

As you start to consider some of the components that need to exist in an enabling environment for your work (which you can still do even if you don't yet know what precise job you want to do), you might want to prioritize the following factors differently from me. In fact, I've not given these any particular order other than to start with people. I'd be surprised if your own ideal environment didn't in some way define the kind of relationships you have with others and the role they play in relation to the work you do.

Sometimes when clients are considering a career change, I suggest that they go and talk to friends and relatives who appear to enjoy their work and ask them what it is they like about their jobs. It is often a source of surprise that one of the first things they mention is their colleagues:

'I work with a really nice bunch of people.'

'They're not just my workmates: they're my friends.'

'I'm part of a team that functions really well.'

I have to say that I was also surprised by this tendency to start talking about colleagues, as I assumed that the contented worker would describe the nature of their work first. Of course, that's an important factor too but, on reflection, I realize that perhaps putting working relationships high on the agenda isn't that remarkable. After all, if you've ever experienced the problems and frustrations caused by a bullying boss, uncooperative colleagues or undermining behaviour, you'll be only too aware of the way that poor relationships with colleagues can undermine your effectiveness and cause a great deal of frustration.

As you think about your needs in relation to other people in your workplace, you can perhaps begin to see some of the ways that they play a crucial role in helping you to function. Yet the people in your working life need to do more than simply *not* be obstacles. Your own working-style preferences will determine how you like to work with others.

- Do you like to be part of a team, or work independently?
- Do you like to get direction from others, or prefer to determine what you do – and how you do it – for yourself?
- Do you need others to inspire you and stimulate your creativity, or are you a self-starter who can get on with the job given a bit of peace and quiet?
- Are you spurred on by being in competition with colleagues, or do you prefer to work more cooperatively?
- Do you find that hierarchical organizations give you a sense of security, structure and place, or do you yearn to work collaboratively in a team of peers?
- Do you see colleagues as nothing more than people you share a workplace with, or do they become your nine-to-five family?

Your answer to each of these questions may not come down clearly on one side or the other; you might like, for example, to have some general overall direction for your work but also the freedom to decide when and how you do it. So the options in each question above are not necessarily mutually exclusive. Nonetheless, I hope that they help you to define for yourself the way in which people you might work with can help you perform at your best and enable you to work in the way that most suits you.

Your work environment is not only created by the ways in which people support you but also the role you play in supporting them. Your fulfilment might come from enabling another to do a really great job. If you've ever watched a Formula 1 race and seen a car pull into the pits for some work, you'll have seen a group of people whose purpose and satisfaction comes from helping both driver and car to do their best. Or what about the manager who prepares a report for the board? Or the PA who makes the travel arrangements for a colleague's business trip? Even the dentist who gives you a filling has a nurse to mix the amalgam to just the right consistency. The work you do may not only be rewarding in itself but because it enables others to be effective.

Colleagues are not the only people who feature in the landscape of a meaningful working life. You might also have some kind of *customer*: patients, passengers or service-users; readers, listeners or viewers; residents, students or clients. If your vocation involves provision of a service or product, what kind of customer do you want to supply and can you describe the sort of relationship you wish to have with them? Once again, the more you can define the way you wish to interact with this group of people, the better able you'll be to consider their place in your work environment and the sense of meaning they bring to it. A youth worker might thrive on the challenge of working with troubled teenagers. A therapist can delight in finding a route through a person's depression. A teacher who is prepared to persist may see the moment when the pupil finally 'gets' it. These are magic moments that can sustain a person's motivation and sense of purpose at work.

Your magic moments don't have to be as dramatic as these. A satisfied and appreciative customer in any context will be a rewarding experience. And even sometimes when the customers aren't, or can't be, appreciative, the time that you have spent with them can have a valuable quality to it.

Amy works in a residential home for people with dementia. Some of the people she cares for struggle to express what they need or to understand what Amy is asking them. With the type of clear verbal communication that most of us take for granted not always available to her, Amy has to find other ways of connecting with people. She's learned to read between the lines and to understand body language. She has a variety of strategies and approaches she can draw on according to each individual's needs, and their form and severity of dementia. With some, she might avoid open questions, offering clear choices instead – 'This cardigan, or this cardigan?' She takes time to understand each person's background and habits so she is better able to anticipate their wants and requests.

Amy values the uniqueness of her relationship with each person, whether or not they recognize her or remember her name. 'This is their home,' she says. 'My job is to help them feel comfortable and get on with their life. Each time a person expresses contentment, or I help calm an individual's agitation, I feel I'm getting it right.' For her, each relationship has a significant quality that she finds hard to describe but knows when it is present.

Who are the people that you would like to feature in your working life and how would you characterize the relationship you'd like to have with them?

■ Physical environment

Perhaps the aspect you most associate with the term *work environment* is the physical space and facilities that you occupy during your working day. Again, thinking about your needs in this respect means removing obstacles to your performance. What are the environmental requirements that allow you to move freely and operate efficiently? What helps you to maintain a good level of performance throughout the day?

Perhaps you subscribe to the 'a tidy desk means a tidy mind' school of thinking. I certainly know that for many people, including myself, having the piles cleared off the work surface somehow enables clearer thinking. But I also know people who like the chaos of piles of books, papers and paraphernalia which create a sort of Hammer films-style tortured genius environment. The messiness forms a kind of cocoon in which to bury themselves in their work, with their seemingly random approach to organization a stimulus for lateral thinking and creativity. Sometimes having lots of piles functions as a visual overview of projects or tasks in hand.

Of course you may not work, or want to work, at a desk. There's certainly nothing natural about sitting hunched over a keyboard and phone for eight hours a day. You might desire a work setting that takes you out of the office regularly – or altogether. Or perhaps you want to work in an office for the first time in your life.

Work can take place indoors and outdoors, standing up or sitting down, in one location or moving around a variety of settings. What appeals to you and what do you feel would help you to perform best? Do you want a noisy and bustling environment, or a quiet, more reflective space? What needs do you have for physical comfort? What equipment, materials or resources would you like to be working with, and what requirements would you need to accommodate them? What helps you to concentrate and bring the best of yourself to the work you do?

Many more people these days are choosing to work from home, at least some of the time if not all week. Not having to commute is appealing and finding some peace and quiet to get on with work uninterrupted can be a boon. For some, though, the idea is anathema; they find it too tempting to lie in, watch daytime television or get on with the laundry. They need their colleagues around them to create a disciplined environment that will encourage them to knuckle down.

Clearly, the nature of your work and your personal working-style preferences will dictate many of the requirements of your work environment but here are some other factors that you might want to consider:

Energy levels

Through the day your ability to concentrate, and the energy you can bring to your work, rises and falls. Your energy levels, unique to you, affect your ability to perform – sometimes quite drastically – and the lows can be exacerbated by both your physical environment and the way you look after yourself (or don't) during the day. If your workplace is stuffy, noisy, cramped, air-conditioned or artificially lit, then your low points may be more marked or prolonged. And if your highs are sustained by the adrenaline of a frantic workplace, supplemented by a high caffeine and/or nicotine intake, they may last longer but will take their toll later. To help minimize the peaks and troughs in your energy levels, you might want a work environment where you can eat well, have ready access to drinking water and can periodically stretch your legs and breathe some fresh air. Even a quiet space set aside for a short nap is becoming a feature of some workplaces.

Flexible working hours

Some folk are morning people; others come alive later in the day. If you are able to work when you are most alert, it is going to help you perform at your best. While impractical in some jobs, other employers can accommodate some flexibility and many now operate flexitime. The self-employed can sometimes structure their day around their bodies' natural rhythms. A two-hour window for starting work can make all the difference to a person's performance. What's your preferred working day? 8 a.m. to 4 p.m. or 10 a.m. to 6 p.m? Or somewhere in between? I know a writer who works best late at night, writing on into the early hours, then sleeping for most of the morning – it's what works for him. His first novel has just been published.

Travel

Some people enjoy travelling to work. It gives them time to wake up and gather their thoughts for the day. Others feel they spend too long getting to and from their workplace, becoming exhausted and stressed in the process. Whether you want to commute or not, how long you want it to take and your preferred mode of transport are all factors that can make the difference between setting you up for a day's work, or undermining your capacity to feel fresh and realize your potential.

I hope you'll also be able to think of some other factors that contribute towards an enabling work environment. Perhaps it helps you if your workspace has some personal touches, something that is an expression of you. Or it is in a place that integrates well with other facilities that contribute to your well-being – near a gym or swimming pool, perhaps, or a good café where you can take time out to think. I had a chemistry teacher who practised his golf shots in the science lab while dictating notes to the class. Perhaps it helped him concentrate. It wasn't dangerous (he used indoor balls) and he remained one of the most highly regarded teachers in the school.

The Brazilian industrialist Ricardo Semler wrote in *Maverick* – his account of turning round a failing business by treating his employees like grown-ups – of the way his factory workers were encouraged to take responsibility for their workspace. 'Soon chaeflera and gibóia plants were sprouting between the machines on the shop floor,' Semler writes. 'Then some of the assembly line workers decided to paint the factory. Each selected a colour for the column nearest him, while the walls behind each group of five or six workers were painted a collectively chosen shade... The plant was closed for an afternoon as workers took up brushes and rollers and turned it into a plant of many colours, including the industrially-unlikely shades of pink and magenta. These hues may have looked chaotic, but they were symbols of our desire to let our workers control their destinies.'

Giving employees control of their work environment in this way was part of a wide range of measures that Semler introduced to give employees greater ownership of their workplace, which in turn increased their commitment, motivation and performance.

Obviously, the line of work you are in and the nature of your employer will determine to some degree the environment you work in. And if you are applying for jobs, there is going to be a realistic limit to how many of the components in your ideal work environment they may be able to deliver. But if you have some clarity about your physical environmental needs, remembering that they will contribute to your ability to work to the best of your ability, it may help to steer you round some choices or prepare some questions to ask prospective employers.

■ Tasks and activities

Another feature of the landscape that makes up your working life is the tasks and activities that you undertake, the very nature of the work you do. Although the activities you engage in may be determined by the skills you want to use, there may also be room to choose exactly the kind of tasks you engage in.

A gardener, for example, may prefer nursery gardening to larger jobs. Sitting on a lawnmower or taking a chainsaw to a hedge is very different to seeding and planting out. Most gardening work involves a mix of these tasks, plus many more. Some gardeners choose to specialize and seek work in an environment that enables them to do so.

If your aptitude is in, say, communicating, organizing or caring, then there is a great deal of scope for thinking beyond your skills to the way that they translate into tasks. As you visualize yourself doing work you enjoy, what kinds of activities are you engaged in? In what ways are you using your hands? Your whole body? What equipment or materials are you using? Even if you are only able to describe these in general terms, you can combine them with what you know about your physical environment and the people within it to begin to shape some idea of the landscape in which you wish to work.

Vincent is rethinking his career. A teacher for over twenty years, he feels he's played out his role in secondary education. With another twenty years to go before conventional retiring age, he feels ready for a second career but is still trying to finalize what that might involve. He knows he wants to continue making use of his skills as a teacher, but says 'I've got tired of the sound of my own voice.' When asked about the sorts of tasks and activities he'd like his future work to involve, he says he'd like to sit down for a change! He enjoys writing and always regretted that he was so pushed for time when preparing materials for lessons, as he felt he could have done a better job if he had not been so stressed. He pictures himself in a pseudo-academic role reading, researching and writing. His house has a room that looks out onto the garden and he'd like to turn this into an office with his desk by the window. Wouldn't he feel isolated? Perhaps he's over-compensating for the classroom environment?

'Are you kidding? When my kids get in from school, that's the end of the isolation. And I could always do some tutoring to keep my hand in. But the work I'd like to do would focus on something I already do but make it full-time.'

Although still trying to nail down exactly what his future work might involve, Vincent is currently exploring opportunities for producing educational resources, writing a book and seeing if his skills are transferrable for use in business training and other educational settings. His search for meaningful work is not being driven by the opportunities already known to him. Instead he's defined the nature of the work he wants to do and has begun to seek out possibilities for meeting this criteria.

■ Maintenance activities

As mentioned previously, working in an empowering environment won't alone fulfil your potential – that is something internal to you. But if you take time to ensure your work environment presents as few obstacles to your performance as possible, you can eliminate significant sources of frustration that may undermine your effectiveness. The more inhibitors you tolerate, the greater the likelihood that your work will be slowed down, sidetracked or blocked. Like an athlete who is trying to race on dry sand, the environment can create such a drag on your performance that it overshadows any sense of satisfaction from work accomplished.

Giving the athlete a firm surface to run on isn't what makes her a great sportswoman. Her natural ability, training, and passion to achieve are the real factors that enable her to win. A good coach, supportive family and excellent training facilities are environmental factors that will help smooth the way by removing errors, self-doubts or inadequate resources. Yet these are not the things that make her vocation successful.

In thinking about your own environmental needs, be sure to recognize where they fit into your overall goal. Yes, it is enabling when your environment supports your work. But it is not your environment that makes you successful – you do. Don't fall into the trap of focusing *so* much on your environmental needs that you lose sight of what you personally need to bring to your work. The people, tasks and physical location that make up the landscape of your working life are only effective if you put the best of yourself in the picture. That not only means honouring your potential but refining the necessary routine, behaviour and discipline that enable you to work at your best.

You need also to take a look at your daily routine. This can be considered a component of your work environment because absence of the right habits (or too many bad ones) creates obstacles to your performance. Thinking about habits dovetails well with other factors we've looked at in this chapter, such as how you work around your energy levels and body clock.

The practices you cultivate at work might help you to get certain tasks done. They may also be ways of keeping yourself physically able to function well. Habits related to sleeping, eating, drinking and exercise are an important part of your self-maintenance. What do you know about the conditions under which your body and mind work best and what habits could (or do) you cultivate that help to create these? Do certain tasks lend themselves to being done at certain times of day? If you are a grumpy morning person, can you schedule, say, meetings until a time of day when you've cheered up? What activities do you tend to become over-absorbed in? Some people only deal with email just before lunch and again at the end of the day, so their replies are succinct and efficient and they are more motivated to disregard any that don't really require a response.

Whatever practices you put in place, they should support your effectiveness. There is no point in finding work in an excellent environment if you turn up feeling exhausted or hung over and then spend too much time on the wrong things. Create some golden rules for yourself that take care of both your physical and administrative needs so that every aspect of your work environment exists to support you in pursuing your vocation.

■ To think about...

1. Who are the people in your ideal work environment and what kind of role and relationship do they have with you and your work?
2. What are you tolerating in your current work environment that is an obstacle to your performance?
3. What kind of physical environmental needs must be met to enable you to function most effectively?

4. What kinds of tasks and activities would you like to be undertaking in your ideal environment?

5. What habits can you create and maintain that enable you to function to the best of your ability?

Six: Finding meaningful work

Wouldn't it be great if there was a computer programme into which you could feed information about yourself and it would cough up your perfect career? Actually, such programmes exist in principle and are now widely used in schools to help pupils make career choices. When my nephew took the test it concluded that social work would be a good career choice for him. Unfortunately it generated the same outcome for most of his friends which rather undermined their confidence in the results.

The problem with these tests is that they can only produce results based on the very limited data fed into them; the job options they describe are not comprehensive. More importantly, they discourage you from thinking for yourself about suitable career choices, feeding the hope that someone else can come up with an answer for you.

I'm not sure it is possible to make realistic choices about your vocation if you divorce yourself from the process of working it out. If you rely on teachers, parents or software to tell you, can you really be sure it is *your* vocation? Because your vocation is an expression of your Self, you need to put something of yourself into the process of seeking it out.

The best computer for helping you identify meaningful work is your brain. It already contains much of the data you need to work out what an appropriate job would be. It is likely, however, that you will have to process some of this data. You will certainly have to add to it.

■ Consolidating your existing knowledge about meaningful work

In the course of this book, you will have already encountered much of the data you need to focus your search for vocation. Having clarity about the values you want present in your work, the difference you want to make, the kind of environment that brings out the best in you, the way you want to express your Self, the tasks and activities you'd like to undertake, the skills you'd utilize and all the other factors you've been thinking about should be helping you identify the key criteria for a meaningful working life. These components of your vocation are already things you were aware of at some level but may have needed to work through consciously in order to understand and articulate them better. In other words, you already had this data to hand but it could have been obscured not only by the way you have been conditioned to think about work but by your anxieties, assumptions and the limits of your experience.

Now is a good time to think about consolidating these criteria. You need to be able to draw readily on them in order to help you focus your search and spot the right opportunities for work that chime with your vocation. A good way of doing this is to draw up your ideal job description – one that incorporates everything you know about yourself in relation to work.

It doesn't matter if you don't know in what particular profession, role or job title your vocation is to be found; this job description doesn't require that information at this stage. This is about compiling in one place all the elements you now know need to be present in your work to give it any sense of meaning. So you might simply head it 'A meaningful job...'

Try to include the following:

- The *values* present in the work
- Your *motivation* to do it
- The *contribution* your work makes
- The opportunities for, and forms of, *creativity* and *self-expression* it involves

- The *skills and abilities* you will utilize – learned, natural and desired
- The relationships you have with *people*
- The right *environment* in which you will undertake your work
- The *tasks and activities* you will undertake
- Your measures for *success*

Compiling your vocational job description like this is a way of consolidating all the existing data you have about the nature of meaningful work for you. It gives you a bedrock on which to build your future investigations.

Which brings us to a really crucial point: finding the right opportunity to match your requirements will necessitate further action on your part. This is about acquiring more data to add to the process of identifying or creating the right work for you.

A large number of people I encounter who are frustrated with their career remain disaffected simply because they do nothing about it. Because the right opportunity hasn't presented itself to them, they assume that it isn't out there whereas the reality is that they haven't discovered their vocation because they have never really looked. This is like trying cook a gourmet dish using only what you find in your cupboard at the end of the month. There simply aren't enough of the right ingredients to hand to make it viable. If all you've ever done is look at the job pages in the paper, hoping to find something good that your experience qualifies you for, you are committing the occupational equivalent of trying to make coq au vin with a tin of sardines and an old Oxo cube. You need to get out there and gather all the relevant resources before you can proceed. And when it comes to finding the right career, the principal resource you need is information.

■ Collecting more information

In effect, you need to set up an investigation. Begin by seeking out the right data to help you focus your search. You are going to play detective and that entails gathering clues.

This will be easier for some than others. You might be one of those people who still does not know what you want to be when you grow up. Or you may have so many ideas that your problem is committing yourself to pursuing one. Perhaps you are somewhere in between, with some inkling about what you'd like to do but not sure if your notion is realistic, achievable or reliable.

It helps if you bear in mind that all you are committing yourself to at this stage is investigating possibilities. You are not making a decision about your future career; you are simply on a case, discovering what can help you make choices and decisions later on. Like a detective, all you can do is start with what you already know.

Having compiled your vocational criteria in your job description, you will have already gathered together in one place much of your existing knowledge about the work you would like. Now you need to take that information on the road to find out who can tell you more about it. Like a detective, you will need to track down witnesses and background information, poking around to see what you can stir up.

It is helpful to start out with a hypothesis to help give your search some direction. Don't worry too much about whether it is right or not, as it mainly gives you a starting point to focus your search for further information. If your hypothesis is wrong, you will soon find out and be able to adjust your search.

When detectives investigate a crime, they look at the evidence to hand, examining the scene of the crime, talking to witnesses and using their existing experience and knowledge to help them proceed. Often they will start with a hypothesis based on what they know at the outset. For example, you can perhaps recall hearing police saying on the news that they are proceeding on the basis that 'the gunman was acting alone'. They make this judgment based on what they know so far and use this hypothesis to make decisions about the way they will proceed with their investigation. As they look into the case in more detail, they sometimes encounter information that changes their original hypothesis. The theory they started out with may have been wrong but it served a purpose in that it got the investigation moving.

So the hypothesis you start out with is important in giving you a springboard for action. As you proceed with your investigation and gather more information, you might revise your hypothesis along the way. Your hypothesis should answer this question: what kind of work will fulfil the criteria you have compiled?

You may already have an inkling about this and, if so, it is time to take it seriously and explore the possibilities. If you've been nursing a secret fantasy to pursue a particular career, now is the time to stop dreaming and start investigating.

If you have lots of ideas but can't decide which to look into first, use your job description to narrow the field. Draw up a list of all the possibilities you've thought about. Then consider each one in the light of your criteria. What are the top three that emerge? You could begin exploring all of these at the same time and see whether you end up more drawn to one than the others.

If you genuinely have no idea, that needn't stop you investigating. However, it is my experience that very few people have no notion of what they want to do, particularly by the time they have pulled together their vocational criteria. More often the sticking point is that they won't take their hypothesis seriously, perhaps through lack of confidence or an anxiety about the perceived risks involved in changing career.

If you can't figure a hypothesis out yourself, a useful exercise is to trawl through the job pages in the paper and pull out any that appeal to you or catch your attention – regardless, at this stage, of whether you qualify for the job. You might also look out for employers that appeal to you, even if the advertised job does not. At this stage, you are simply using the job pages to help you identify some possibilities for research or to spark off an idea about where to start your investigation.

■ Identify your 'witnesses'

There are two types of witness with whom you can start discussing your desired vocation – expert witnesses and casual observers. The experts will be people like careers advisers, HR managers, outplacement consultants, recruitment agencies and so on. In some cases they will offer a conventional approach to careers advice, telling you what your experience and qualifications would enable you to do or about the jobs they are trying to fill that you could try. Not all of them will hear what you have to say about your requirements for *meaning* in your work. But the better ones will listen and offer their insights as best they can. Whatever their response, I think the conversations are worth having.

Expect to gain something useful from every person you approach. Your expert witnesses are not going to hand your career to you on a plate but they can offer you valuable *leads* – nuggets of information that help to direct the next stage of your investigation. This could be information about the state of the job market, suggestions about professions or jobs that you weren't much aware of before, organizations that it might be worth exploring, ideas about books, websites or training, contacts to get in touch with and so on. These are all clues that you will want to follow up to see where they take you. Don't be tempted to dismiss what they say – every lead is worth pursuing to see where it goes and what new information it yields. Periodically you'll reach a dead end. Try to let this happen only when the trail runs cold rather than because you are jumping to conclusions about the value of exploring it further.

Your other witnesses are your casual observers. These are the people in your existing network of friends, colleagues, family and acquaintances. All of them have experience and knowledge of work and can share ideas and insights with you. Become adept at describing to others what meaningful work is for you and sharing your criteria with them. As well as being able to tell you about the job they do, each person in your network also knows lots of other people in a wide variety of jobs. By taking time to tell them what you're looking for, you are inviting their suggestions for jobs and professions they know about that meet your criteria – and hopefully they can put you in touch with relevant contacts so that you can expand your investigation.

If you already have a fairly clear idea about the type of work you are looking for, it is obviously going to be a much narrower quest, focusing on talking to others who already do that job, researching any necessary training or getting in touch with relevant professional bodies.

If your career hypothesis involves setting up a business or going freelance, your investigation is also going to include getting advice about developing a business plan, securing finance, marketing yourself and so on. The government's Business Link agency is a good place to start with this.

Perhaps you are thinking all this sounds as if it is going to use up a lot of shoe leather. You will certainly need to be prepared to commit time, perhaps over a period of months, to your investigation. A fulfilling career is not worth compromising on and a great many people's unhappiness with their work stems from their expectation that a good job should be easy to find. They neither take the time to explore their own motivation and requirements nor to research the right opportunities out there. They end up making do with whatever comes to them easily.

Suppose you accidentally shredded a jackpot-winning lottery ticket; you wouldn't hesitate to commit time to rummaging through the bin for the bits and patiently piecing them together – the effort would be worth the reward. Isn't a vocation more deserving of some time and attention in order for you to get it right?

One thing I have noticed with clients who begin investigating a career change is that they seldom take long to find the field of work they are going to focus on. Even those who proclaim at the outset that they have no idea what else they could do soon find that they turn in a new direction and are able to go forward successfully. This reinforces for me that the greatest obstacle people encounter in finding work they want is that they don't really spend time looking for it. Workers understand a great deal more about themselves than they sometimes realize and often need only a little extra confidence or determination to find a working life that is truly fulfilling. For those who take their vocation seriously, simply setting out to investigate possibilities can quickly open up new horizons or make vague dreams reality.

■ Is your vocation staring you in the face?

One of my favourite music websites is CDbaby.com which features recordings by artists of all genres (and a few that defy description) from independent labels. The site was set up by Derek Sivers, himself a musician, who was frustrated at how difficult it is to get your music distributed unless you are with a mainstream label. He decided to set up his own website and offered to sell some of his friends' recordings alongside his own. He has now sold over one million CDs, generating US$ 10 million in revenue for the 70,000+ artists featured on the site. The website is easy to navigate and customers can listen to sample tracks online before buying. Their approach to customer service is personal and efficient, and the tone of the website is suffused with quirky humour from Sivers and his team. This is not just another faceless enterprise; they've listened to every CD they sell. There is a real sense of the people and purpose behind the business. You also get to discover some really great music you won't find on your high street.

I like the CDbaby story because it demonstrates one of the ways that people find new directions in their work – by resolving problems that block their progress. Rather than letting an obstacle remain in their way, they set out to create a solution for themselves and others. It seems to be the experience of many that the vocational destination they set themselves is not where they end up. In the process of setting out on the journey, they discover a better place to go, one they could not have foreseen at the outset.

Some people's careers have taken a new direction as a consequence of encountering a need that wasn't being met. Many charities have been created on this basis. Paulette Balcombe, for example, founded H.O.P.E. when she discovered that there was very little support or information available to help her deal with the panic attacks she'd been experiencing. Now the organization she founded provides exactly the kind of services she originally wanted.

A change in personal circumstances can also be the spur to help people find their niche. This was the case with Candy Verney, whose story was featured on *Home Truths* on BBC Radio 4. Formerly a schoolteacher, she needed to find a way to earn an income when her marriage broke up. Reluctant to return to teaching children, she decided to start a class, 'Singing for Beginners', at the local adult education college. She had always been a collector of songs and felt that this was something she could offer. She puts the emphasis on ensuring that people have a really good time in the process of learning to sing. For her the thrill is helping people who believe they can't sing to discover that they can. She now teaches over 100 people a week (some of whom are in their seventies) and her class members testify to the way they feel transformed by finding their voice and fulfilling a long-held ambition.

What Paulette and Candy have both managed to do is see the opportunities around them. Although neither of them would necessarily have chosen the circumstances in which they found their new working life, they were alert to the possibilities their situation created for them and responded accordingly. Both used what they knew about to create new roles for themselves and there is clear evidence of the difference their work makes to those who use their services.

Could it be that you are facing such an opportunity yourself? Is there a vocation staring you in the face that you could pursue if you had the confidence and self-belief? A common attribute of many vocational workers is that they are prepared to get their sleeves rolled up and get on with it, surmounting the personal doubts and anxieties that can accompany a career change. Whether you are overcoming an obstacle to your progress, a personal crisis or simply needing to change work through force of circumstance, be alert to the possibilities that are around you and seek out the potential for creating meaningful work from the ashes of personal difficulty.

■ Testing out possibilities

In the same way that it is sometimes difficult for adolescents with no work experience to make informed choices about their future, you might equally struggle to identify with a new field of work if you have had no opportunity to test the water. It is sometimes a useful part of your investigation to give it a go and see how you get on. Obviously, you might not want to commit yourself to giving up your existing job on a whim so finding some way to test drive a new career that fits around your existing work is desirable.

If you have a contact who is already in the field of work that you are investigating, you could explore the possibility of doing some work-shadowing where you take a day or two to accompany the person as they carry out their job. Even a visit to their workplace and a chance to talk to a few other colleagues could be helpful to your research.

If there is an appropriate training course, evening class, self-study programme or workshop that would give you a chance to explore some of the skills or knowledge required in your proposed career, seek it out. Such training opportunities are valuable not just for any certificate or qualification they provide but also for testing your degree of interest in and engagement with the topic or skills. It is the process of learning that counts here, not the outcome of the training.

There may not be a course that fits exactly with the field of work that interests you but even something that is loosely related can be of value in helping you test the water. Taking a course that explores a proposed new line of work can be very effective in helping you try a new direction without having either to give up your existing job or to commit yourself to anything.

A more lateral way of using training to help you uncover your vocation is to take courses that interest you and then see what possibilities for further training and employment they lead to. With this approach, there is no need to start out knowing what work you are investigating. Instead, you can use a course that is attractive to you as an avenue that you can explore. This is a more intuitive way of moving forward and can be really effective for those who struggle to identify a hypothetical job at the start of their investigation.

Another good way of pushing forward your research on vocational opportunities is to do some voluntary work. Again, there may not be a chance to do exactly what you want. Nonetheless, it is still possible to find a volunteering opportunity that gives you a flavour of the work you are investigating.

I recently met someone who is considering training to be a counsellor. Before committing herself to the lengthy process of qualifying for this role, she is going to work as a volunteer for a telephone helpline. Although the helpline does not offer counselling, she will be trained in both listening skills and ways of asking open questions. These are both elementary skills that counsellors use. She will also gain an experience of working one-to-one with people who are seeking help and support. So although her voluntary work is not a direct experience of the work she wants to do, it has some parallels. If she isn't suited to the helpline, she probably won't pursue training as a counsellor.

Even working in a voluntary but unrelated post can help clarify your thinking about your vocation. Putting yourself in a new situation that draws on different skills and abilities widens your horizons. It is all useful experience which can test your motivation and shed new light on your skills in a situation where you know your work makes a real difference. By putting yourself in touch with new people and opportunities, you expose yourself to other influences and possibilities that can provide you with new leads. Many people even find new work directly as a result of volunteering, having become engaged in the cause or issues that their efforts support. Others find that volunteering opens their eyes to the needs of other people in such a way that their own problems are refocused, enabling them better to appreciate their own situation. The joy of voluntary work is that you can never predict the impact it will have on you. I have listed some websites at the back of this book that can point you to volunteering opportunities in your area.

■ Take your dreams seriously

Jack is an officer in the British army. His career has spanned twelve years and has seen him accrue an excellent service record, rapid promotion and an impressive display of medals. But the military wasn't his first career choice. He graduated from university with a degree in botany but in the course of pursuing his Masters degree had a bitter encounter with the academic world and crashed out in a bout of depression. Turning his back on botany, he signed up for the army, which has been largely a rewarding experience.

However, the war in Iraq has challenged Jack's political viewpoint and he has reached a point where he wants to move on. He says he doesn't know what else he wants to do. It is clear that his interest in botany is undiminished and I sense a tinge of regret that he left that field of work behind, even though he has no regrets about his army career.

When Jack says he doesn't know what he wants to do, he is being somewhat disingenuous. After a bit of questioning, it emerged that he has, for many years, pondered the idea of running his own garden centre at which he would also run botany classes and provide a landscaping service. Asked why he had taken so long to mention this, he started to backtrack. 'Oh, it's just a stupid idea. I could never make it work. It's too risky. I don't know anything about running my own business. The world already has too many garden centres.'

Yet it is clear that Jack has been living with this idea for a long time. This is not just a passing notion he has vaguely toyed with but an idea that he has refined and developed in his mind over the years, visualizing how it would work and what it would feel like for him to run a business he felt passionate about. He can describe in some detail how his business would function, the different aspects he would develop and some ideas that would be utterly unique to it. But rather than face up to his business idea, he gunned himself down with negative assumptions and defeatist self-talk. In the next chapter, we'll return to Jack and look at how he turned around his outlook on the future and formed his idea into an action plan.

Jack's story is another example of someone who nurtured a secret fantasy, yet was almost embarrassed to admit it to me. It fuels my suspicion that a greater number of people who say they don't know what they want to do for a living actually know very well but let their anxieties and doubts crush their dream before they even explore it.

Jack doesn't have to commit himself to anything to begin investigating whether his idea is practicable. He doesn't need to leave the army to begin researching the market for garden centres. Gathering information is not a career move. Before closing down an idea, take time to discover whether your doubts are well-founded or just spring from a lack of self-confidence.

I think people have two sorts of dreams: literal and figurative. Jack's is a literal dream, in that it is rooted, fully-formed and entirely realistic, in what he knows. Others have figurative dreams, where they fantasize about doing something different but the fantasy is vague, fanciful and incomplete. A former colleague and I, in moments of high stress, used to daydream together about new jobs – she to waitress in a café, I to work in a bookshop. These dreams grew out of a reaction to our current situation and a desire to escape from the pressures of a strategic and proactive workload that was trying to squeeze more creativity out of us than we felt able to give.

I actually pursued my bookshop fantasy one quiet summer, when I worked odd days to provide holiday and sickness cover for staff. I loved being there and worked with wonderful colleagues who did all the complicated bits. I just sat behind the till reading their books, serving customers and changing the CDs on the hi-fi. And they paid me for that! It provided the perfect contrast to the other work I'd been doing but I also knew that working in a bookshop wasn't the sum total of what I wanted to do in my working life. There were other projects I wanted to pursue, other routes to finding fulfilment.

Figurative dreams still have something to tell you about your aspirations about work. I was able to recognize that my bookshop fantasy incorporated a number of insights about my career aims; that I wanted to spend less time working proactively and balance it with some reactive activities. And that I wanted a working life which allowed more time for both reading and writing; that I was stressed out and needed space to just 'be'. By getting under the surface of a figurative dream, you can often gain important insights about your desire for a different working life which the dream does not express literally.

Whatever you daydream about doing, take it seriously. Take time to unpack what the dream is about and think about how you can give your work fantasy tangible expression. Think through what holds you back from taking it seriously. If you are not the daydreaming type, here are a couple of useful exercises you can try:

1. The Charity Fantasy – suppose you are given the job of starting a new charity, with unlimited funds to do your work What charity would you set up? It could be related to art, sport, religion, children, health, animals, the environment, international development – anything you want. What impact would you like to make?

2. The Inheritance Fantasy – an unknown relative dies and leaves their fortune *and* their genius IQ to you, their sole heir. The only stipulation is you must keep on working. What would you do? Is there retraining through which you would fund yourself? What job would you take on, or what business would you set up, regardless of your current ability, talent or limitations?

These exercises give you a chance to play with your deepest desires about work while removing the sorts of limitation we often impose on ourselves that stop us pursuing our vocation. Your answers may be literal. If they are figurative, you may want to reflect on what they tell you about the nature of meaningful work for you. An apparently unrealistic daydream may still be translated into a workable context. Examine your ideals until you find a way of expressing them in the real world.

■ To think about...

1. Prepare your description of meaningful work as suggested and practise telling others about the nature of the work you are looking for.
2. Hypothesize about the sorts of work that will meet the criteria in your job description, and use this to start your investigation.
3. Identify suitable experts and contacts with whom you can begin discussing your investigation
4. What opportunities for trying out a new line of work through training or volunteering could you explore locally?
5. What dreams do you have about work, and what do they tell you about the nature of meaningful work for you?

Seven: Overcoming barriers to change

It is one thing to feel disaffected with your career but quite another to do something about it. As we've already seen, a significant issue that holds people back from seeking a more fulfilling working life is that they simply don't know what else they could do. Yet even those who *would* like to explore other options often stay in their rut rather than take action to resolve their unhappiness.

Why is this? After all, if one encounters a problem in life, it is normally second nature to seek a solution. Yet when it comes to careers, many choose to stay fixated in the headlights of their unhappiness than to hop off the highway into better territory.

Because your work makes up such a big proportion of your waking life, and because you've been groomed to prepare yourself for the workplace from a young age, meddling with your career on your own terms can understandably feel pretty scary. It is easy to let fears, anxieties and poor self-belief get in the way of claiming the fulfilment that you seek. And given that decisions about your work to date have often been in the hands of others (will you get the job you want? will you be accepted for a place on the course you choose? will you be supported by your parents in pursuing your dream career?), it is easy to begin to divorce yourself from any sense of ownership or responsibility about the direction of your career.

In this chapter, then, we will look at some of the common hurdles workers face in taking control of their careers and in pursuing jobs that offer the motivational rewards they seek.

■ Myths and fears

There are a number of factors that discourage people from taking their vocation seriously that are connected to particular beliefs they might hold about themselves in relation to their work. These include a commonly held myth about duty, a fear of being self-indulgent and false assumptions about the possibility of success in making changes.

The myth of duty is part of an older mindset that says you must simply stiffen your resolve and get on with the work in hand; work is not about your own satisfaction but rather about meeting your responsibilities within society, paying your taxes and earning money to support your family. The myth of duty says that you should not expect to enjoy your work but simply do your best as a citizen or responsible member of the family. When you have been conditioned to believe this myth, it is easy to assume that nobody really likes their work This is a seductive view to cling to for those who hate their jobs. Wouldn't it be maddening to know that while you are grinding away doing something you hate, other people might be out there enjoying themselves in the workplace. Much safer to assume that everybody else dislikes their work too.

A variation on the myth of duty is a fear of self-indulgence. This fear tells the person that they shouldn't be pushing themselves forward, navel gazing or trying to better themselves. Such behaviour is deemed to be selfish and too full of one's own importance. You should know your place and stay in it.

This anxiety about putting oneself first sometimes crops up in the caring professions where there can be a conflict between balancing your needs with those of people you assist. Given that such work is about meeting the needs of other people, it stands to reason that you shouldn't think too much about your own.

Over the last five years, I have done a lot of work with Anglican priests and some of them really give this fear house room. Having accepted their vocation, some clergy (though thankfully not all) feel they have to put the needs of others before themselves to such an extent that they end up too stressed, exhausted and (often) depressed to take care of anybody. By neglecting themselves, they undermine their ability to meet the needs of their parishioners.

Every priest (like any worker) has a unique set of strengths, along with a vision of the difference they would like to make. If they are to meet the terms of their vocation, they will need to play to these strengths, focusing on issues that matter most to them. For example, I have met many priests who started out knowing exactly what kind of parish they wanted to work in but, rather than aiming for a post that suited their calling, they have been talked into accepting the wrong job to satisfy an incalcitrant bishop. In addition, they have felt that they must be available to all people at all times. As a result, they spread themselves too thinly, doing too many things that they were not equipped to handle.

As much as any other kind of worker, clergy are at their best when they play to their strengths and work at the things they enjoy most. But a fear of self-indulgence stops them from focusing overmuch on what they excel at, undermining their effectiveness and happiness in the role. Acting in your own best interests should not be confused with selfishness. If your vocation is about serving others, you can probably do more for them by fulfilling your potential than by staying in a job that fails to take advantage of the best you have to offer. It's like what they tell you on in-flight safety announcements when they demonstrate the oxygen masks: sort your own out before trying to help anybody else, because you won't be much use if you are asphyxiating.

■ Unbolting your assumptions

Another classic trap people set for themselves is to make myriad assumptions that persuade them that fulfilling their potential is impossible.

Maya, who is 39, wants to leave her job and go back to university to take a degree in a field she has long wanted to study. 'But I couldn't go back to student poverty again,' she says. 'I've grown too comfortable with my lifestyle.' So she dismisses the idea. Yet she is assuming that returning to university would mean three years of no money. It is not an unreasonable assumption for her to make: she has been to university before and done the 'whole student thing'. She doesn't have much in the way of savings she could use. So for her to dismiss the possibility of returning to university is understandable. But wrong.

Maya lives in a house that she bought 15 years ago. Since then it has increased in value by nearly £200,000. That's a *lot* of equity to be sitting on. Because she let her assumptions get in the way of some systematic and structured thinking, she didn't explore the possibility of using that equity to fund her through university. Neither had she looked to see what job opportunities – and potential income – she might have after graduating nor what loan facilities would be available to her as a mature student. In short, she shot down any chance of doing what she really wanted because she didn't notice what assumptions she had bolted onto the notion of returning to university.

We all do this, of course. The older you get, the more your life experience informs your view of the possibilities in front of you. You use that experience to help you assess the likelihood of succeeding in a particular course of action. Unfortunately, the information you draw on is usually outdated because it relates to the past and not the present but your brain is very good at subconsciously assessing your chances based on past performance. As a result, it is easy to make 'logical' yet wrong assumptions that cling, limpet-like, to your thinking and sabotage your judgment.

Finding a way forward often necessitates spotting the assumptions that are ingrained in your thinking, then unbolting them so that you can take a long hard look.

■ Overcoming your objections

At the end of World War II, many members of the armed forces, anxious about life after demobilization, worried about whether they would get jobs at a time when so many others were leaving the forces and looking for work. Some were concerned that their wartime experience didn't equip them for a good job, others that the routine of a nine-to-five job would seem dull after all they had been through.

One officer at the time, stationed in Asia, was the actor Dirk

Bogarde, who edited an army newspaper. Aware of the anxieties that beset returning soldiers, he wrote an editorial on the subject which is described in John Coldstream's biography of Bogarde:

Someone said the other evening, 'You know I dread going home on demobb [sic]... I'll never get a job,' and we have probably heard that remark about fifty times a week from people out here in the army... During the war years they learned a good deal about life, which should help them, they also learned a lot about themselves, which should also help them a bit... they learned about their fellow men, and were faced with heavier responsibilities than they had ever had to cope with during the years of their civilian life... If a man has a personality there is little that he cannot do. That has been proven over and over again. If he is aware of himself, and aware of what he can and cannot do... and will take the trouble to learn from people, he has made a start. We have all striven for our Freedom, and now, when so many of us have it within our grasp, we baulk at it and are afraid to go forward and take our opportunities with open hands. The world is as full of jobs as it is of fools... there are a thousand chances waiting if you have the courage enough to seek them out; courage, hardness, determination, and personality. If you say 'I will!' who's to stop you?

Although it perhaps reads something like a pep talk, Bogarde's piece pinpoints some important issues for anyone who lacks confidence in seeking meaningful work. He speaks of the value of self-knowledge in marketing yourself. He mentions that bringing your personality to bear will help you fulfil your potential; that you may have to think laterally about your experience to date and how to apply it in a different setting in future; that you should maintain a willingness to continue learning; and that finding the right opportunity for you may require courage and sustained effort.

Overcoming any negative self-talk or doubts that creep into your thinking when considering a change of job or career is something of a mental battle. It is often necessary to face them head on and work away at overcoming them in order to progress towards the kind of work you seek.

One person who has been doing this is Jack, the army officer discussed in the previous chapter who had for many years nurtured the idea of running a garden centre. When it came to considering how to realize this project, he came up with a number of objections that were based on unexamined assumptions and badly-drawn conclusions. He could, like people often do, have left it at that – assuming that his pre-existing knowledge and assumptions were enough to enable him to make an informed decision. But Jack recognized that the objections he raised were somewhat hollow, rooted not in fact but in his anxieties about failure. As he began to examine his objections, he was able to turn them around by using an effective questioning approach, based on the premise that every doubt contains an important question. Seeking the answer to that question will assist your career development in a practical and constructive way. Jack's objections, you will recall, were as follows:

- It is just a stupid idea.
- I could never make it work.
- It is too risky.
- I don't know anything about running my own business.
- The world already has too many garden centres.

These are typical of the sorts of reasons people give to justify why they can't fulfil their potential or pursue their vocation. Most of them are stated in very general terms which is a clear indicator that they are based less on fact than on personal doubt. By identifying the question contained in each objection, Jack was able to move away from feeling thwarted in his ambition and begin to take some action:

It is just a stupid idea
If it is so stupid, why has it stayed with me for so long? What more, if anything, could I do to make it a great idea?

I could never make it work
What are the skills and qualities I possess that would enable me to make it work? Who do I know that could help me with the bits I'm not so hot on?

It is too risky

What exactly is the risk? What do I need to learn about this market to enable me to judge the risk effectively? Where could I go for this information?

I don't know anything about running my own business

What skills and knowledge do you *actually* need to run a business? Which of these do I already have? Which others could I learn? Who do I know who could help me on this?

The world already has too many garden centres

Where is there a gap in the market for a garden centre? Where would some of the unique ideas I have for a centre give me an edge over competitors?

Taking time to write your objections down on paper allows you to look closely at them, assess what assumptions you might be making and turn them around into a question to investigate. Jack is now currently exploring the world of garden centres, assessing the potential for his idea. The great thing is he has not had to commit himself to anything – he is still in the army but, rather than merely worrying about his future, he is now able to focus on the way forward. The more answers he finds, the more questions he will uncover to add to his list. But each question becomes a jumping-off point for the next part of his investigation and, as he works through them, he'll begin to gain real clarity about where he heads next .

I'm sure Jack has what it takes to make his garden centre a success. But even if he decides that it is not feasible, he will be making that judgment from an informed standpoint rather than from his nagging self-doubt. He won't have to live with himself wondering 'What if...?' for the rest of his life.

◼ Applying for jobs

For many people, there is nothing more certain to inflate their insecurities and anxieties than the process of applying for a new job.

This is not surprising, considering the kind of scrutinizing, testing, probing and invasion that candidates have to undergo. Even if you only fleetingly doubt yourself, you can be sure that the prospect of seeking new work will hasten the effect. Every weakness, shoddy exam result, bad career decision or unfortunate episode will loom large to confirm that you must be mad to entertain getting such-and-such a job. Just forget about it. You haven't got the experience they are looking for anyway. Or the right qualifications. An interesting job like that? Why would they give it to someone like you? No, there will be much better people applying for it. Pity, really, because it appears to be exactly what you are looking for...

Without even getting hold of a job description or application form, or casting an eye over one's CV to check it is up to date, thousands of people flick through the job pages of the newspaper every week and talk themselves out of pursuing jobs they like the look of. So it is time to nail down some of the unhelpful thinking that inhibits people seeking new work:

I haven't got the experience or qualifications they are looking for

Bear in mind that when employers advertise a post and state the experience or qualifications they require, they are often talking about their *dream* employee. In many cases, the person specification will have been written to describe the vacating post-holder, so it defines someone who was so good at the job they were able to advance onto something else. In reality, employers end up recruiting the person who comes closest to meeting their criteria. If you don't apply, they are probably only going to appoint somebody else who didn't have all the stated experience or qualifications.

I don't understand everything on the job description/advert, so I obviously couldn't do the job

In fact, lots of people who write job descriptions and adverts have no idea what they are doing. Really. You might think that they are written by 'highly trained Human Resource management professionals', but in many cases they are written by the person who will line-manage the new employee, and they are not always very good at clearly expressing and defining what a job is about on paper. And even when job descriptions are written by HR people, this is no guarantee that they will make sense. Arguably, the opposite is true. Too often, they are written to be understood *within* the organization and not by outsiders. If you come across unfamiliar jargon or terminology, don't assume you are not up to the job. Be aware that some bosses will be trying to make bits of the job sound more interesting than they really are, so they devise tortuous and pretentious phrases to describe an activity that is a lot more straightforward than it sounds.

I'm not sure I really want this job

The only time you need to decide whether you want to do a particular job is when you are offered it. If something has caught your eye about a particular opportunity, then follow it up, even if you have some reservations. You might find that these are unfounded or that they can be resolved at a later stage. Never assume that an advertisement for a job necessarily tells you all you need to know in deciding whether to pursue it or not.

Filling out this application form is like taking an exam

Indeed there is a lot about the employee selection process that can trigger those old exam feelings. As you work through the application form or your supporting letter, you might well feel, as someone said to me recently, 'Will I score enough points to pass the test?' Even when an employer has given clear criteria for applicants, don't fall into the trap of simply telling them what you think they want to hear. If you are going to find a job that fits you, it is vital that you convey something of yourself to them. By referring to your own list of criteria for meaningful work, you can talk about the ways you believe their job offers what you are looking for in your working life. Your application shouldn't merely aim to tick all of *their* boxes but should convey something of the real *you* in the process. By bringing this kind of authenticity to your application, you will convey more about yourself in a clearer three-dimensional way. It will also help you to think through whether the job is really for you, because you are bringing your own needs into the process and not merely trying to please a prospective employer. Don't be afraid to be yourself because, if they don't like you or your motivational needs, you won't find fulfilling work with them anyway.

I'll never get a job I like. It is always the same old boring ones that are in the paper

That's because not all available jobs are advertised. There is growing evidence to suggest that it is a minority of workers who find jobs through the newspaper. One firm of outplacement consultants recently tracked the way their clients found new work. The vast majority (over 70 per cent) found work either by speculatively contacting companies or through networking. Less than 10 per cent found their next job in the paper. While these figures will vary considerably for different industries and professions, they do go to illustrate that being proactive in defining the work you want, then seeking it out, is still an effective way to find meaningful work. Keep tabs on the news within your field of work to find out who is hiring, merging, investing, launching, restructuring, piloting, expanding, and so on. By taking time to read papers and professional journals or to attend conferences, you are taking responsibility for finding out where new opportunities lie.

■ Overcoming your inhibitions to change

There is no shortage of objections you can throw in the way of making a change. You can tell yourself you are too old, or too inexperienced; that a change would be too risky, or unrealistic. Provided you recognize that these are not facts but insecurities, you can find a way to move beyond them. In particular, facing up to a change in your working life will be made easier by sticking to three golden rules:

Build on your success

When Tim Henman reached the semi-finals of the French Open tennis championship in 2004, an unparalleled achievement for him, he talked about the way his new coach had helped make it happen. 'He told me to stop overanalysing my game and to focus on what I'm best at.' Henman's coach understood the way that our heads can go into overdrive and dwell too much on the wrong things – mistakes, insecurities, lack of confidence and so. Focusing on your strengths and achievements will do much to help you shut down the noisy chatter in the back of your mind and get on with the job of fulfilling your potential.

Define success on your own terms

It is vital that you have a clear vision in mind about the working life you want to have and that this is centred on your deepest aspirations. As soon as you allow others to dictate your measures of success, your commitment to achieving your goals will dwindle because your heart is not in it. It is not always easy to stake your claim about the kind of career you want to build for yourself, particularly when it runs counter to received wisdom amongst your friends, family and colleagues. But only you can define meaningful work for yourself. If you are going to rise above your anxieties, doubts and objections, you must be committed to a course of action you genuinely desire.

Prepare to persist

I once met a school janitor who was unbelievably lucky in winning competitions. He reeled off a list of holidays, cars, bicycles, kitchen appliances, televisions (five) and other prizes that he had won over the years. Was this the luckiest man alive? No. Simply the most dogged. He won lots of prizes because he entered lots of competitions. He got his head down and took the time to enter anything that came his way. He didn't allow the times when he won nothing to put him off. Seeking work you want may require the same dedicated effort from you. Don't expect to land the first interesting job that comes along. Take time to develop and refine your criteria, then press on with networking, applying and investigating. Stay focused on your goal and be willing to put time and energy into achieving it.

■ To think about...

1. What holds you back from exploring a new direction for your work, or even a career change? What *negative self-talk* do you indulge in which discourages you from taking action?

2. What assumptions are you making about the difficulties in pursuing the work you want? What could you do to test them?

3. What objections do you raise to discourage yourself from pursuing a new work idea or job? Write them down and turn them into questions to create a plan of action.

Eight: Work, money and pensions

In the wake of Christmas 2003, British consumers were more than £109bn in debt. And that isn't counting mortgages – just credit cards, overdrafts and loans. Forty per cent of adults have racked up an average debt of nearly £6,000 thanks to their flexible friends. (It is worse north of the border where half of my fellow Scots have about £8,000 of personal consumer debt – the worst in Europe. Still, doesn't it make a nice change from hearing about our record levels of heart disease, alcohol abuse, bad diet...?)

Clearly, there is an array of social and economic factors that have contributed to such runaway consumerism. Not least of these is what used to be referred to jokingly as retail therapy. These days it is an expression that has lost its ironic edge as the nation heads for the shops every time it needs cheering up. Had a family argument? What you need is a new pair of shoes. Feeling a bit grumpy? Take home a new DVD. Bad day at the office? Get a bottle of wine and a ready meal and put your feet up.

If the work we do is not satisfying, we naturally look elsewhere for our contentment. When we're not enriched by what we do from nine to five, then of course we'll switch our attention to the evenings and weekends to satisfy us. And, increasingly, what we want to do in our spare time costs money. Even an evening at home in front of the television will, for many, involve flicking through dozens of satellite channels on a state-of-the-art plasma set. A 'cheap' night in can cost a fortune these days.

Holidays, socializing, entertainment, sport and fitness, days out, the car we drive, the home we live in (and its extensions) have become the focus of many people's lives. While there's nothing wrong with these things in their own right, if the emphasis on them is too strong, this may be indicative of a lack of any fundamental sense of fulfilment. Spending money on distractions is used to compensate.

Karl Marx called religion the opium of the people because he believed it was designed to take the minds of the poor off their oppression. These days it is consumerism that creates an illusory fantasy of happiness when it becomes the primary focus of someone's life. If your work serves only to provide you with a means of funding whatever takes your mind off how much you hate your job, then you really are caught in a trap. The more you dislike your work, the more you'll seek to compensate with your lifestyle. Yet there is always more to acquire – a bigger house, a better car, a faster computer, more gadgets in the kitchen, more fashionable shoes, more exotic and exclusive holiday destinations.

It's an insatiable appetite because there is always something more to aspire to. No matter how much we spend on our lifestyle, if we fail to care for our innermost need for fulfilment, no amount of consumption will fill the void. It is easy to see how so many people rack up big debts.

■ Vocation and money

People with vocational careers have a different attitude to money. It is not their income that is driving them but their need to satisfy their sense of purpose. Their lifestyle doesn't compensate for a job they don't like but complements a working day that is in itself motivating and rewarding. Sometimes they are extremely financially successful, too, and enjoy the benefits of a comfortable home and lifestyle. But these things don't take centre stage. It is as if they are enjoyed out of the corner of their eye – fringe benefits that are appreciated but aren't critical to their sense of success.

Their fulfilment is internal, rooted in a strong sense of self and a clear purpose in their work. It's not what they own that tells them they are successful: they measure success in terms of their professional objectives. Whatever lifestyle and possessions they have may be enjoyed as a tangible reminder of that success but they don't cling to these things the way rampant consumers do. They know that their capacity to succeed lies in following their vocation.

Others who work vocationally may just have enough to get by on but are quite happy with that. Their interest in money and lifestyle extends only as far as ensuring they've got enough to allow them to get on with their 'work'. Their environment is good enough to enable them to do what they have to do; they have enough to pay the bills and take care of their responsibilities. If they are committed to a cause, this may lead them to share what they have with others or donate their surplus to others who need it more.

Although there is room for flexibility in attitudes to money on the part of vocational workers, it is significant that money is not regarded as inconsequential. It is necessary not only for their own care but also for their family responsibilities, allowing them to do their work without too much friction. While money and spending does not take centre stage in their lives, neither is it regarded as unimportant. They view finances with sincere responsibility and will give time to ensuring their financial affairs are in order. While they neither ignore the need for money and its place in their lives, it is not seen as the key outcome of their work either. It flows from their work but they see their work as having a different outcome – the difference they make.

■ Regarding money incidentally

The relationship that vocational workers have with money is similar to a performer's appreciation of applause. When a concert pianist walks out on stage, her primary focus is not the audience or how loudly they will clap at the end of the performance. If it were, she would limit her repertoire to crowd-pleasing, lowest common denominator, pieces of music. But she knows how dissatisfying this would be, how much it would limit her repertoire and how quickly audiences would become bored with her. So the pianist wants to honour her craft. Her mind is focused on playing well technically as well as giving expression to the music she is playing. She will want to explore new forms of composition, as well as give her own distinctive interpretation of the classics.

Yet it would be ridiculous to suggest that she is so focused on her musical objectives that the reaction of the audience is of no importance to her. She doesn't seek applause in its own right but it has incidental importance as it is an affirmation of her talent and an acknowledgment of her achievement. It gilds her accomplishment and is a measure of how well her reputation is growing which in turn will enable her to do greater and better things.

It is this incidental approach to money that I see in people who are focused on their vocation. Jobs are not chosen because of how much they pay but how well they fulfil the person's need for self-expression, creativity and meaning. A vocational mindset puts the work first because through it success is achieved – not merely money and status but accomplishment itself.

The economist John Kay has coined the term 'obliquity' to describe the idea of achieving goals indirectly. The most profitable companies, he says, are not those that are most profit-orientated. Where a business is focused on innovation, service or technical solutions, for example, they commit to these goals first and foremost and profits are the by-product. But the income doesn't generate itself; there still needs to be sound financial management.

I was struck by the parallels between Kay's description of obliquity in commerce and the way that I have seen vocational workers relate to money. They don't put profit first either, instead having clear goals that relate to their vocation and sense of purpose. It is an approach to money that can be seen in the following 'Tale of Two Siblings'.

Edward and Susan were born two years apart. They both went to university and got good degrees and they are both married with two children.

Susan trained to be an English teacher and soon progressed rapidly into a senior teaching post, running the English department in a top-performing comprehensive. She married a college lecturer and they used their combined income to secure the best possible home they could afford. After initial renovation work on their home they have continued to enhance it over the years, each time pushing their borrowing requirements to the limit.

Their children are now at university and Susan and her husband are working as hard as ever. Susan is deeply committed to education and passionate about the accomplishments and welfare of her pupils. Like so many teachers, she works much longer hours than she is paid for, struggling to keep on top of bureaucracy, an ever-changing curriculum and declining discipline amongst pupils. Recently her health has started to suffer and she had a short break from work due to stress.

Susan and her husband love their home and spend most of their free time there, rarely going away during the holidays. Their priority is to keep earning as much as possible so that they can continue to enjoy their existing lifestyle and support their children through university. They keep careful control of their finances and are hopeful that early retirement will be available to them in the next ten years or so, but this is uncertain.

Susan's brother Edward studied medicine at university and qualified as a doctor – as did his wife whom he met at medical school. They were both politically active with a particular concern for the injustices they felt that underprivileged people – at home and abroad – had to battle against.

Edward's term as a junior doctor was not only typically exhausting but was enough to disillusion him about medicine as a career. He felt the culture was too competitive and over-managed and he found the hospital environment claustrophobic. Ultimately he and his wife agreed that they weren't making the kind of difference they had imagined when they chose their careers.

They each decided to take a career break and volunteered in sub-Saharan Africa for two years in a medical capacity. When they returned home, Edward's wife had a baby and she chose to stay at home to look after their new daughter and involve herself in the local community. There was a large African population in their neighbourhood and she was able to use the language skills she had picked up when working abroad.

Edward got a job with an NGO, co-ordinating medical services and projects that allowed him to draw on both his medical knowledge and his overseas experience. He got the occasional opportunity to visit developing countries and muck in with the work there. Edward's wife returned to work after their second child started junior school. When the children were small she did voluntary work in the community which opened the way to her becoming a project worker in Health Education. They now have two children, one of whom is at university and the other on a gap year in South America.

In many ways, Edward and Susan's lives are virtually indistinguishable. Both chose what are traditionally considered to be vocational careers – teaching and medicine. Both married and raised families. They own their own homes; they are able to support their children's further education – and both take care of their own finances.

The differences only become clear on closer scrutiny. Edward's view of work is driven from a very different place to Susan's. Susan and her family have focused on squeezing the maximum standards of living from their income. They sought to use everything they worked hard to earn to create a space away from work where they could forget about it. They worried constantly about the future, about how they would support their children, cope with a serious illness, manage if the house needed a major repair and whether they would have enough for an early retirement. In many ways their fears and anxieties as well as their material aspirations determined their career choices. When Susan was offered promotion she didn't think twice about accepting because of the extra income it would provide, even though she much preferred being a full-time teacher to being part-teacher/part-administrator. She is counting the days to retirement and constantly fretting over the bank statements and bills.

Edward was much happier to adjust his lifestyle to satisfy his vocational needs. He put finding meaningful work that was in tune with his values at the heart of his career decisions. When he realized his first choice wasn't going to be a good fit, he made a shift until he got it right. His work was driven by the difference he wanted to make and the feelings of accomplishment he wanted to take home at the end of the day. While it wasn't always plain sailing he never lost sight of the inherent motivational rewards that his work provided and as a result was able to weather both periods of stress and financial pressure without losing heart. Like Susan, Edward and his wife took good care of their financial affairs. But because they didn't need to spend money to compensate for unhappiness at work, or derive their sense of success from the size and décor of their home, they were able to set aside sizeable amounts of money for contingencies and their children's further education. In short, it was easier for them to be content with what they had because of the fulfilment their work provided.

It is this difference in focus that makes Edward such a good example of obliquity in action. He achieved what he wanted professionally and was still able to take care of his financial commitments. While Susan felt trapped in a job she couldn't afford to leave, Edward always knew that he could change at any time if his current job no longer met his need for meaningful work. And while Edward's household income was less than Susan's, it was she who felt most hard up. Her finances were tight because she pushed spending to the limit, while his were comfortable.

What both Susan and Edward illustrate though is that whether you seek money head on or obliquely you still need to manage your finances responsibly. Even if making money is not the main driving force behind your work, you still have to make time for responsible financial management.

■ Financial awarenesss

It is not possible to give serious thought to money in relation to work without understanding the state of affairs in one's personal finances. Indeed, I meet people who feel constrained by financial pressures when they are in fact much better off than they realize – they have simply got into a habit of pigeonholing their relationship with money in a particular way.

Take Maya, from the previous chapter, who thought she couldn't afford to go back to university in spite of owning large assets. Because she was both vague about her financial affairs and had got into a habit of thinking about herself as hard up, she had remained in a career she really disliked.

As someone who normally has to be dragged kicking and screaming to deal with money matters, I'm hardly a role-model in this matter. What I can tell you is that a good deal of financial heartache is caused by ignorance. People simply do not put the numbers together to get an overview of their spending patterns, or devise any kind of budget against which they live their lives. In such circumstances it is easy to get a false impression of your financial affairs. Whether you are one of the nation's debtors, optimistically charging more and more to your credit card, or whether you are a pathological poory like Maya, feeling trapped by needless financial uncertainty, the solution is simple:

- Log your spending
- Prepare a budget
- Get a financial adviser and/or debt counsellor

When people begin looking for a way out of an unhappy career, the prospect of trimming back on a lifestyle they have come to rely on can be a real challenge. If you've become accustomed to spending money to compensate for a lack of fulfilment at work, being told you might have to cut back can be a bitter pill to swallow.

■ Swapping materialism for fulfilment

It should be noted that for many people the way forward with their work doesn't involve reducing their lifestyle or their responsibilities for others. But it does sometimes require being prepared to put it at risk. It certainly requires taking the earning of money from centre stage and setting it on one side. For some, this is too much of a challenge. I've seen people stuck in jobs they hate because they can't let go of their prestige home, sports car or exotic holidays.

It reminds me of a story I was told as a boy about the way hunters trap monkeys in the jungle. They put a nut inside a clay pot that is too heavy for the monkey to carry. The monkey puts its hand inside the pot and grabs the food but then can't get its fist out of the pot. Not willing to let go of the prize, the monkey is trapped and the hunters are able to move in and capture it.

You don't have to look far to see why so many people have a tendency to put money at the core of their thinking about work. For many, financial insecurity is a harsh reality. It is a luxury to be able to ponder and take action on finding more fulfilling work. For those who are living hand to mouth, simply earning enough to pay the bills and eat is the sole focus of their daily existence. It is only when your daily needs are met that you can begin the process of satisfying other needs. In Abraham Maslow's hierarchy of needs, *self-actualization* (meaning to fulfil your potential and be all you can be) is the final level of fulfilment after you've taken care of your physiological, safety, social and status needs.

It is something of an indicator about our relative wealth and quality of life that so many of today's workers are looking to satisfy that final need to self-actualize. It is one more difference between this generation of workers and the last that we are even in a position to consider this. Yet if workers have been so successful at meeting their more basic needs, why do so many of them get caught up in endlessly generating an ever-increasing amount of money? That is to say, if you've proved that you can look after yourself, why do you need to keep on proving it – why would you not feel able to take a risk and reach out for a more enjoyable line of work?

Fulfilling your potential requires you to break out of a way of thinking about money that previously served you well. When you were focused on meeting your more basic needs – for food, clothing, shelter, security and so on – you needed to know the money was going to be there. You developed a way of thinking that encouraged you to see money as a solution and the generation of it as the main purpose of your work. However, money only solves the needs lower down your hierarchy of priorities. It doesn't satisfy your need to self-actualize. Nonetheless, chasing the pay rise is a hard habit to break. It would certainly explain a spending boom among people who are looking for something that money can't buy.

The required shift in thinking means setting money to one side as an objective in its own right while continuing to manage it well enough to meet your basic needs. Only then can you really be free to give unfettered attention to creating a vocational working life. This is not just another variation of the 'money can't buy you happiness' cliché. Money itself really doesn't bring happiness but it can certainly solve some problems that either ease your worries or free you up to focus on your vocational goals.

The point is that the amount you need to satisfy those basic needs is probably far less than you imagine. You don't have to be rich to enjoy vocational work. But you may need to ensure that some basic financial needs are catered for before you can begin to step out in a new direction.

That could mean waiting until the children are a certain age; saving for retraining or – if you are freelance – putting aside limited time to do work that is lucrative if not very rewarding. For those workers who have a portfolio of activities that generate income, there may need to be bread-and-butter money coming from somewhere. This is one of the exciting aspects of portfolio work – that much of one's time can be spent on something you love, funded by a smaller proportion of lucrative work.

For others, however, pursuing their vocation is genuinely lucrative. They have achieved obliquity to such an extent that their vocation is successful both on its own terms and financially. It is not hard to understand how this happens – if you are truly fulfilling your potential, of course you will be successful and in many occupations professional success is handsomely rewarded.

Even stinking rich vocational workers don't bask in their wealth in the way that those who crave money do. Because their success has come from being true to themselves, from their passion and purpose, the real rewards to them are not financial. That they can be well off is a bonus but not an end in itself.

This begs the question: how do you measure success? A few years ago I attended a seminar by Thomas Leonard who asked the audience to complete the sentence 'I know I'm successful when...'. He didn't want one ending to this but at least ten. Once you've mentioned money (if indeed you even do), you are still left with a lot of other things to think about, and it is a great way to uncover your own attitudes and beliefs about success and bring them to the front of your thinking about work. Try it out and see what you come up with.

■ Retirement

Christine has been a domestic cleaner for the last 30 years. Last year, at the age of 68, she decided it was time to hang up her duster and retire. Retirement for her meant telling most of her clients that she would no longer be cleaning for them. She asked the remainder if she could reduce her visits to once a fortnight.

This didn't sound much like retirement to me – so why is she still working?

According to a survey carried out by the Prudential, one in four pensioners are returning to work because they cannot afford retirement. This was quoted in ongoing panic-stricken media reports of current and projected trends that suggest many more of us will have to work well into our sixties and seventies. There is some discussion about whether the retirement age should be moved to 70. Of course, this angst is based on an assumption that work isn't something enjoyable and that retirement is the only attractive escape. There is no doubt that for many people this is the reality and for them to have to continue working because their pensions are inadequate is indeed a tragedy.

But gloomy predictions that we need to work after retirement age fail to take into account the reality that many older people *want* to work. And this is the real reason Christine is choosing to carry on. She is not being forced to continue work because she can't afford to stop, although she admits the extra money will come in handy. The real reason she has chosen to retain a few clients is because she enjoys it. She's always been active and doesn't want to stop now. She likes the social contact her work brings her and the clients she is retaining tend to be the older ones, those who need her most and to whom she knows her work makes a real difference. She is also extremely good at her job, having a reputation as a hard-working and reliable cleaner. Continuing to work means she will retain an active role and a sense of purpose in her later years.

Pre-retirement courses, provided by many employers for staff who are about to hit bus-pass age, emphasize that staying active, building a routine and finding purposeful and productive activities are the key to survival. That needn't mean having a job but it does sound a lot like it.

In fact, many retired people are already very active. Volunteer programmes in the charity sector sometimes rely on older people to form the backbone of the work they do (indeed many volunteer coordinators – often young people – don't capitalize enough on the potential that older people offer). Other retirees are busy caring for grandchildren so both parents, or single parents, can go to work. It is not as if working during retirement is a new idea.

Therapist Fiona Hall, in her newsletter, recently recounted the story of Dave who has been gardening for 63 years.

'He first went out as an enterprising twelve-year-old with a spade and dug his neighbours' gardens for a few coins, or a cup of tea and a sandwich. Enough to pay for the cinema, and a bonus bag of chips if he'd had a good week.

'Ten years past retirement age and he's still working seven hours a day. He's been looking after the same private gardens for twenty years now – when he started they were just a bare patch of earth. He took me to see them and they were stunning; acres of shrubs and flowers, hedges, trees and lawns, all currently placed with an eye for colour, size, texture and overall perspective.

'Dave has never earned very much from his work, he's never been "promoted" or been given a company car. His employers rarely appreciate all the different jobs necessary to keep the gardens looking wonderful. As he said, "They'd only notice if I stopped doing them for a few months."

'He works because he *loves* to. Because he's still learning. Because he has high standards and takes pride in seeing the results. Because a robin has recently taken to perching on his wheelbarrow and getting a free ride. Because he loves to stand at the top of the gardens in the morning and look out over them and suck in their beauty.'

Ken Dodd, once asked when he was going to retire, said, 'People retire so that they can stop doing something they don't enjoy and start doing things they do. I already do something I love, so why would I want to retire?' This quote played on the mind of a client of mine so much that it compelled him to give serious attention to where his career was heading – he wants to be able to say the same.

There are plenty of other examples of people who've continued to work beyond normal retirement age:

- Sir John Gielgud was 95 when he acted in his last film role.
- Actors Lauren Bacall and Paul Newman were still working on the other side of their eightieth birthday. And Gloria Stuart got her big break at the age of 88 and was Oscar-nominated for her performance as the older Rose in *Titanic*.
- Veteran broadcaster, Alistair Cooke, continued recording his weekly *Letter From America* until a few weeks before his death at the age of 95.
- TV presenter Alan Whicker made his most recent television series at the age of 79.
- Pianist, composer and conductor André Previn was Music Director of the Oslo Philharmonic Orchestra at the age of 75.
- I recently saw jazz pianist Dave Brubeck perform at the Royal Festival Hall at the age of 82. The previous year I had seen another jazz legend, Ahmad Jamal, at the Barbican – he was just 80. And while we're on the subject, the Cuban jazz pianist Ruben Gonzalez, who continued performing until his death at the age of 84, once said, 'I have never liked sitting at home doing nothing.'
- French singer Sacha Distel made his West End stage debut at the age of 68.
- Writer, broadcaster and politician Sir Clement Freud was still a panelist on *Just a Minute* at the age 80.
- Dr Henry J. Heimlich, who gave his name to the technique for saving someone from choking, continued to work on methods for saving lives until well into his eighties.
- Nobel Peace Prize winner Dr Norman Borlaug, who developed high-yield pest resistant crops which have saved millions of lives in Africa and South America, continues to work today. He came out of retirement in the 1980s in response to the African famine at that time.

Surely all these people didn't continue working because they were hard up? Of course, these are all examples of people who were successful – which is rather the point. People who do work they enjoy, excel at and which is appreciated by others are less inclined to retire than those who feel ground down, exhausted and bored by their career. If your work really does connect with a deep sense of purpose and vocation, would you really want to stop at the age of 60?

It is clear that we could use a new model for later life, not just because we're an ageing population with a pension crisis but because the possibilities that exist now for an enriched third age are greater than ever before. Today's 60-somethings are healthier, fitter and less burnt out than their parents were at that age. Their life expectancy is much longer and they have greater energy than those of earlier generations.

Charles and Elizabeth Handy, in their book *Reinvented Lives: Women at Sixty – a Celebration*, have captured this new age of possibilities in a series of 28 essays by women entering their seventh decade. The stories they tell include many examples of women who, at the age their mothers retired, are reinventing themselves to pursue new vocations, education or relationships; or who simply feel that their existing work is coming to its most fruitful and rewarding phase.

My own encounter with someone starting a new chapter of their career in later life takes the form of Meryl Doney, a writer who, in her late fifties, changed gear to pursue new work in the arts. Like many women of her generation who left school not really knowing what they wanted to do, she trained as a secretary. Following jobs in advertising, media and the arts, her abilities as an able administrator and project coordinator quickly took her into more varied fields of work, and when a former colleague set up a new publishing company Meryl went with him, eventually becoming comissioning editor.

The new company had a good idea of what they wanted to produce but needed to establish a stable of authors. As a result, many of the early titles were written and developed in-house. This enabled Meryl to begin a writing career and to develop a particular specialism in designing craft and activity books, as well as writing books about faith and religion for use in schools. Some of these early books remain in print today, having sold millions of copies around the world. The themes of both creativity and spirituality that have been present in her writing since the seventies offer an insight into where she would take her work later on.

When Meryl and her husband were expecting their first child, she continued writing on a freelance basis, something she was able to fit around family life, and she has continued to write for children ever since. When both of her own children were at school, she was invited to return to the same publisher to create a new line of gift titles, a job she did for seven years. With eligibility for the state pension just around the corner, Meryl could easily have stayed in her job just a little longer until retirement age. Instead she embarked on two new careers, both of which were sparked off by key conversations.

The first conversation was with her husband. Every year he and Meryl set aside a day to take stock of their lives, family and relationship. In 1998, with a small surplus of income at their disposal, their annual reckoning focused on a powerful question: 'Is there anything we haven't done yet that we've always wanted to do?' As it happened there was and, as her husband went off to buy a horse, Meryl set up *The Art Room* – a project to find new ways to promote artists using, for example, their home as a gallery. This venture led to her being invited to curate a major touring exhibition, a project that was three years in the making and, barely over, now has Meryl thinking about her next curating job.

The other conversation was with a friend who was setting up a marketing department for a major London gallery and wanted Meryl on the team to take responsibility for research. She now works there three days a week and her writing and curating take up the rest of the week – often she works into evenings and weekends.

I asked Meryl, now in her early sixties, if retirement is a concept she contemplates. 'I've always been someone who believes it is important to make your life count, and there is still one unfinished strand of work that would pull together different threads of past work. I've long felt that people with a faith should be more visible in the arts, that there is a real capacity for art to communicate important issues and to enhance life. I'd love to see the establishment of a spiritual centre for visual arts in London.'

What would make her slow down? 'Well, you need to balance your health with the contribution you want to make. Mind you, I have more energy now than I did when I was being a "mum". And it's such a buzz being at the centre of the arts in London with lots of exciting things going on.' Meryl's energy is tangible – she brims with enthusiasm, with a smile you could measure in watts, as she strides briskly to the table where we have a cup of tea and sandwich together overlooking the Thames.

Meryl's working life is another example of someone who has a portfolio of work that makes up her career. She has a strong sense of purpose about the contribution she wants to make and the fields of life she feels passionate about. Her ability to renew her career on the threshold of 60 came not only from this but also her practice of regularly reviewing where her life is heading and taking action to keep it on the course she wants for herself. Her story reflects some important themes for those who want to keep growing and developing in their work. She kept her networks alive and many of the opportunities that came her way arose because she'd maintained contact with old colleagues and friends over the years. Even when at home with the children, she made an effort to stay interested in the outside world.

She also kept pushing herself to learn. When Meryl returned to work after having children, the culture of the workplace – and the technology being used there – had really moved on. She took time to get to grips with it all so she was up to speed with those around her. 'It expands your mind no end,' she says. I think this kind of ongoing curiosity and willingness to keep learning is a key part of staying creative, imaginative and fulfilled. Meryl's decision to keep on working is driven by her love of the work itself and her enthusiasm for the projects with which she is involved.

Rather than buying into the media's gloomy predictions of an impoverished old age, wouldn't it be better to take hold of a vocational working life and carry it on for as long as it is fulfilling and rewarding? It needn't mean full-time work but the possibilities for building consultancy, freelance or portfolio work around the traditional pursuits of old age mean than your senior years could continue to be purposeful, active and vocational.

■ To think about...

1. What role does money play in your work-life balance?
2. How well informed and organized are you with regard to your financial affairs?
3. How much money is enough? What do you need to meet your responsibilities and live comfortably?
4. How do you define *success* in your working life?
5. What have you not yet done that you've always wanted to do? What is stopping you, and what do you need to overcome such obstacles?

Nine: Making the most of your current work

Finding meaningful work doesn't always involve changing your job. One reason disaffected workers sometimes struggle to identify an alternative career is because they are already fulfilling their vocation. Indeed you may have reached this point in the book and realized that you really are in the right job for you – particularly if you've been working through the questions at the end of each chapter and found the answers consistent with your current work.

Career disaffection occurs not only when a worker is in the wrong job but when there are workplace obstacles that hold them back from fulfilling their potential. The frustration of someone who is in the right vocational job but feels obstructed in undertaking it properly can be just as strong as that felt by someone who knows they need a career change.

Clearly there are all sorts of issues that might cause such obstructions. I've found four that seem to crop up particularly often with clients:

- I'm not motivated/I'm lazy
- I have difficult working relationships with my colleagues/boss
- I don't have enough time to do everything
- I don't feel confident/can't say 'no'

What all of these have in common is that they hinge on how you see yourself and feel you are regarded in the workplace. Depending on your mindset, these sorts of issues either help to cultivate a blame mentality ('it's all *their* fault') or they provide a mental playground for your anxieties and doubts to have a field day ('it's all *my* fault').

Of course, the reality is that these kinds of obstacles to meaningful work are not specifically anybody's fault – they arise from the unique interaction of individual workers with their environment. In order for them to cease getting in the way of your performance, you may have to tackle them both practically and psychologically. To do so may require you to take the initiative in sorting things out rather than hope that someone else (whose job you might think it is) will do it.

■ I'm not motivated/I'm lazy

People usually feel bored when they are not motivated. Yet the people I've noticed who seem most upset about feeling demotivated are those who are in jobs they love. It can be a source of some confusion to be in a job that should be fulfilling, yet feel disengaged and off the boil. In reality, many people have cycles of energy, engagement and creativity in their work; sometimes a loss of these things may be nothing more than your body's way of telling you to slow down and just cruise along for a bit. There's no law that says you should be able to operate at full stretch all of the time.

More intriguing, I think, are the reasons that people ascribe to their lack of motivation. Chief among these is blaming oneself, in particular saying 'I'm just lazy' or 'I lack self-discipline'. These self-accusations are hard to verify and are not convincing when they come from the mouths of people who have achieved much and work hard. But when such people find it difficult to engage with their work, they jump to the conclusion that it is somehow their fault.

Laziness is a particularly unhelpful concept. It's an entirely subjective judgment that doesn't help you move forward in solving the problem – it just writes you off as somehow inherently flawed. While (arguably) there may be some people who are genuinely bone idle, the laziness that many people ascribe to themselves is there for good reason. What they are really talking about is *avoidance*. In struggling to engage with a piece of work or an area of activity, it is a constructive starting point to ask yourself, 'Why am I avoiding doing this?'

If you can identify the cause, you're ready to begin thinking about what you need to overcome your avoidance. Common reasons for people shunning work are:

- Feeling stressed
- Being tired
- Anxiety about failure
- Lack of confidence in personal ability
- Distraction by other concerns
- Lack of support
- Lack of time
- Lack of access to necessary resources
- Contribution is not recognized
- Fear of rejection or confrontation
- An unpleasant task

Nicholas is in charge of corporate communications for an energy company. He manages a good team of people who are hard-working, creative and fun to work alongside. He feels he has really found his niche and hopes to stay in his post for several more years. Lately, though, he's been feeling lacklustre and has been idling along. Although the work still gets done, he admits he's only doing the bare minimum and tries to get home as early as possible. What has changed in his job?

'Nothing,' he says. 'We're still doing the same kind of work, but somehow I'm not engaged in the same way.' Has he changed? 'I don't think so. I still believe this is the best job I could be in and on paper it covers all the things I'm looking for in a job.' Perhaps he's just having an 'off' period and needs a new challenge to reinvigorate him, I suggest. 'Mmm, maybe...'

It finally emerges that Nicholas's company is undergoing a restructuring, following the enforced departure of the Chief Executive under less than clear circumstances. Furthermore, the new Chief Executive will not be in post for another four months. Nicholas comes to recognize that his disengagement has been brought about by a number of concerns that he has not previously articulated. The company is in a state of flux and it is uncertain what the future holds. He realizes that it is hard for him to get excited about current projects given that they may become obsolete amidst organizational changes. He also doesn't believe the board should restructure until the new Chief Executive is in place, as he thinks the new postholder will want to have input into that thinking – and will perhaps make further changes when s/he settles in. Nicholas's work objectives are tied to a plan conceived by the now discredited Chief Executive so it is hard for him to remain committed to them.

In this light, his demotivation makes perfect sense. Is the work he does now going to come to fruition? Indeed, will he still have a job once the new structure is in place? Nicholas now understands that he's been feeling at a low ebb because these question marks are hanging over him. In short, he's actually undergoing a form of stress – not the sort that comes from frantic overwork but from a lack of integrity in his objectives and an uncertainty about whether his efforts will accomplish anything.

Only by examining the reasons for avoidance can you begin to plan a way forward. Nicholas began to refocus his work on those areas that would have either an immediate impact or where he was certain they would result in long-term benefit for the company regardless of future strategy and structure. He also learned to give himself permission to operate in a lower gear than he would normally – recognizing that his reaction to the uncertainty of his future was perfectly normal and that sometimes the best thing he could do was to go home on time rather than work late.

If you find you are blaming yourself for being lazy or undisciplined, take time to ask yourself why you are avoiding what you need to do. Try and pinpoint reasons as specifically as you can and then use them to plan how to overcome the obstacles to your performance. As well as identifying what you need to do for yourself, consider what you need from others and ask them for it. Although lack of motivation is a state of mind, the solution is often not psychological but practical. Working through the problem in this way can begin to create tangible solutions that help to get you back on your feet.

■ I have difficult working relationships with colleagues

All of us, from time to time, have to work with colleagues or clients who we find difficult. Personality clashes, irritating habits, values at odds with our own or power politics can leave us feeling stressed, angry and upset. Given that we can't 'zap' such people out of existence (no matter how much we might fantasize about it), how can we work alongside people who simply rub us up the wrong way?

A useful exercise is to sift out those aspects of the person's behaviour that actually cause you a direct and observable problem and separate them from those things that are merely annoying. If a colleague, for example, misses an important deadline, it may lead to extra work for you, added pressure or costly rescheduling of the project. If a client cancels an order or skips an appointment, then you may face a financial loss. These issues are the tangible evidence of their behaviour and you can tackle them in two ways:

1. Confront the individual with the effect that their action has had on you and discuss with them how your problem can be resolved and what can be done to avoid it occurring in future.
2. Plan some strategies for solving the problem that the person's action (or inaction) has caused you.

Tackling the issues in this ways allows you to stay in the driving seat and, instead of feeling a 'victim' of their behaviour, gives you a way of moving forward constructively rather than simmering with frustration at them. As well as the tangible problems that your colleague's behaviour or action causes you, it is likely that you may also be feeling irritated or frustrated. While these feelings are understandable, they exist only within you. Perhaps you see their behaviour as symptomatic of a 'bad attitude' or 'typical of them'. Whatever the case, it is helpful to distinguish between what is merely annoying or discourteous behaviour, and the real problems that arise from it.

I remember a manager getting cross with an employee who, from time to time, would announce that she was taking a day off in lieu of extra time worked. Although the employee was up to date with her work and wasn't required to cover for anyone, the manager felt disgruntled that he hadn't been asked for permission. In this situation, taking time off caused no tangible problem but the manager was irritated by what he construed as a cocky and disrespectful attitude.

In these kinds of situations, it is often most useful to find a way of dealing with the irritation without recourse to the colleague. Feeling annoyed is your problem and may well be based on a subjective judgment – after all another person might not find the colleague or client's behaviour annoying in the slightest. Find a way of letting go of the feelings, or resolving them, and move on. As it happens, the manager in the situation above chose to ban his employee from taking a day off 'just to remind her who is the boss'. In doing so, he turned an internal annoyance into a tangible external problem because he needlessly alienated and demotivated his employee.

Using this two-step approach can be very effective at liberating us from the frustration caused by people we find hard to get along with. Like many exercises, it is worthwhile taking time out with a pen and paper to jot down the issues arising from a colleague or client's annoying behaviour, and list the tangible problems (external) in one column and the associated feelings (internal) in another.

While working through practical solutions to problems caused by a colleague is fairly logical, dealing with the difficult feelings they cause can be messier. A missed deadline or task that hasn't been completed properly, for example, can leave you with a practical difficulty to resolve. However, a thoughtless word, lack of consideration or show of temper may not cause an actual work problem but can still leave you feeling angry, upset or hurt. Such feelings are not only difficult to cope with but can also undermine your effectiveness – feeling furious at someone's behaviour can significantly inhibit your performance and creativity. If you face such a situation, here are some strategies you can try.

First, see if you can break the pattern of your emotional reaction. When someone has annoyed you it is easy to feel that you're a 'victim'. You may not feel comfortable with the strong feelings that the person's behaviour has brought about in you and so may try to justify them.

Typically this can result in fretting about the situation, replaying over and over in your head (or in hushed conversations with colleagues) the reasons why you feel upset. Unfortunately, this seldom leaves anybody feeling better and serves instead to intensify the emotional reaction.

Anything you can do to break the pattern of fretting is helpful. Common solutions involve counting to ten, taking some deep breaths or going for a walk. These are good strategies if they work for you and can help to disconnect you from strong emotional responses. Relief, though, is often temporary and you may have to repeat the technique. This is not a failure but merely an indication of the strength of your emotional reaction. Persist with whichever strategy works best for you.

It might also sometimes help to give the 'offender' the benefit of the doubt. Once someone has really annoyed you, it is easy to begin expecting them to do it again. You begin to keep watch for their next offence. Such expectations only serve to reinforce your negative feelings towards them and inflate your sense of being wronged.

Everyone makes mistakes and it is perhaps unfair to judge other people too much in the light of theirs – as if it is only their faults that define their character. There may even be room for a little forgiveness. In his remarkable book, *The Lost Art of Forgiving*, Johan Christoph Arnold says, 'When we forgive, we not only pardon a failing or a deliberate act... but we also seek to rehabilitate and restore [the person responsible]. Our forgiveness may not always be accepted, yet once we have reached out our hand, we cleanse ourselves of resentment. We may remain deeply wounded, but we will not use our hurt to inflict further pain on others.' Forgiveness is one F-word we should probably use more often in the workplace. When we feel unable to forgive, we carry a grudge with us that prevents us from moving on.

While we're on the subject of forgiveness, it is worth asking yourself if you have anything to apologize for. Did the person purposefully set out to annoy you in a conscious or premeditated way? It's easy to feel that they did (especially when we're playing the victim role), but it can really help to give them the benefit of the doubt. Would their action annoy others as much as it annoyed you, or is it a personality clash? Is their behaviour a reaction towards something you did or said?

Another helpful approach is to try to put yourself in the shoes of the person you struggle to get along with. If you could see the situation from their point of view, would it shed new light on their behaviour? What do you know about the other person that could explain the way they behave? If you don't know much about where they are at, there may be a case for sitting down and trying to get to know them better. It's only when you begin to understand the other person's point of view that you can make sense of their behaviour.

A useful way of building bridges is to ask some open-ended questions of the other person to find out more about how they're feeling about work, or whether there are any ways that you can support them or take pressure off them. Showing an interest in this way can build trust and help you to see beyond the everyday interactions you have with them.

■ Managing your boss

Coping with an annoying colleague is arguably never harder than when that person is the one who is calling the shots. Whether that person is your line manager or, perhaps, a key client, it may not seem so easy to be proactive in smoothing things over if you feel that they hold more power than you. As well as the strategies above, there are some particular approaches that you can use with a boss who is impeding your performance. It will serve your interests if you can manage this relationship in such a way that you are not only better enabled to perform your role but that you support her in fulfilling hers.

The process of managing the relationship with your boss hinges on having a clear understanding of your mutual needs and being able to openly communicate these. It is easy to assume that, because power traditionally lies in the hands of one's 'superiors', it is up to your boss to make all the right moves here. But the strategies below rest on the assumption that, if you take the responsibility for building up the working relationship, you will support your own fulfilment and achievement far more than he can ever do.

Anticipate your boss's needs. Delivering what she needs from you before she even asks for it will build her trust in you. This is a particularly powerful strategy when your boss is inclined to tell you what to do rather than work it out with you in collaboration. By delivering not only what is expected but also what your boss needs – before she's even realized it herself sometimes – you take the need for you to be told what to do out of your boss's hands. So if she's left with little to say in terms of giving instructions, there's more space for her to seek your opinion or listen to your needs.

Help your boss see the whole picture. He's busy with his own workload as well as with those he is responsible for overseeing so he can't see everything. Don't assume that he understands what your needs are – or even that he ought to be able to. Take time to explain your needs to him and help him understand what information and support he can give you that will help you to do your job well.

Offer solutions instead of problems. If she's busy with her own workload, the last thing she needs is you coming up with a load more problems. 'But that's what she's paid for, isn't it?' In a sense, yes, but if you want to build an effective collaborative relationship with your boss it won't help if you're always expecting her to work things out for you. Taking problems to the boss encourages her to act the role of answer-giver – which discourages her from being a listening and consulting boss. And if you're taking problems to her too often she'll begin to see *you* as the problem. She's then more likely to impose solutions on you, whether or not you were seeking them in the first place.

When a problem situation arises that you feel your boss needs to know about, go into your meeting armed with two or three solutions. This way you demonstrate your problem-solving capabilities while at the same time keeping your boss up to date with the situation – you'll be more likely to have a peer-to-peer discussion than a teacher-pupil one.

Offer solutions as a negotiation tool. Listen to the problems your boss is complaining about. When you know and understand the pressure points and frustrations that he is experiencing, you can use these as bargaining chips to get the support or behaviour you want from him.

This is a strategy that involves waiting for the right moment. If, say, a boss has a tendency to behave in a strongly directive and controlling way, wait until he's complaining about the pressure he's under before offering to take some work off him. Here you are encouraging him to delegate at the point where he is most likely to see it as a solution to difficulties he is facing. Follow up by taking responsibility for the supervision process by suggesting the points at which you'll report back on the work or the circumstances in which you'll seek his help. By taking the initiative to map out this process, you reduce the need for him to feel that he needs to keep checking up on you.

The management writer, Peter Drucker, suggests going to your boss periodically and asking, 'What do I do... that helps you do your job? And what do I do that hampers you and makes life more difficult for you?' Take the initiative to resolve the problems you face, or meet the needs you have, rather than waiting for your boss to act. Don't wait to be asked for information, updates on your progress or even for offers of support. See it as your own job to make sure that you get what you need to perform at your best, and then deliver 10 per cent more than is expected of you.

One final thought while we're on this topic – accept your boss's quirks and idiosyncrasies. Rather than expecting your boss to conform to some photo-fit ideal of the perfect manager, accept him for who he is. Observe the way he likes to work and fit in with that. Assess his strengths and weaknesses and then adapt your own behaviour and performance to complement his. You'll avoid getting hung up on your expectations of how he should relate to you and instead be able to work on building a better relationship, based on the reality of the situation.

■ I don't have enough time to do everything

'Time poverty', as it is now fashionable to call it, is blighting many people's lives, not just at work but also at home. There isn't the space here to explore the subject of time management in any real depth so I have listed some recommended reading on the subject in the appendix.

I have a couple of observations to make, however. The first of these is that there is a widely held mythical belief about efficiency. There is a limit to how much work can be done in a day and a point is reached where you simply can't fit any more tasks into the available time. Why then do we inflate our expectations about working faster if we're already going at full pelt?

We suffer from a concept of efficiency that is not appropriate for many of today's workers. The idea of efficiency is that output is maximized within the time available. It's a concept that works well on, say, a production line where tasks are predictable and repetitive. The chances are, however, that you do your job at a desk, not on the factory floor. If your work involves problem-solving, creative or strategic thinking, communication, service delivery or new initiatives, you will be engaged in a much broader range of less predictable activities. Your performance is not about how much work you do but how effective you are.

Much of this kind of work needs space to flourish. Cramming the day with tasks, activities and meetings will cramp your ability to think imaginatively and creatively, which in turn undermines your ability to be fully effective. When you feel yourself slowing down, letting your mind idle or engaging in distracting activities, it may not be that you are lazy or inefficient – simply that your mind is putting the brakes on you so that you are better able to process the problems and issues you face. But it's hard to feel good about letting this happen when there is a ton of work to be done.

Making the most of your time may not be about working harder but about making better choices on how to use your working day. If you feel you've reached the point where there is more work than you can ever realistically undertake, don't give yourself a hard time about being inefficient or unproductive. Reduce the load instead and *delegate, automate* or *eliminate* some of it.

Delegate

I guess more of us would delegate work if we had someone to pass it on to. The flattening of organizational hierarchies, an increase in PC-based self-administration and the rise of home-based freelancers means that even those who once had people to pass work on to no longer do. Delegation may be fine for the boss with a PA or the head of a department but the rest of us can only look on in envy, can't we?

Actually, I think there's more scope for delegation than we realize – particularly if we're prepared to see the boundary between our professional and domestic lives as being flexible. Rather than seeing 5.30 p.m. as a hard and fast border between two competing spheres of life, try seeing all of your tasks and activities for both home and job as your 'work'. By giving equal weighting to the things you have to do at your desk and those at your kitchen table, you may find it easier to take your need for help seriously.

By taking this flexible view of your working life, you have more choice about when to do pieces of work – paying some household bills when you're at the office, say, or using quiet time late in the evening to finish writing a paper or report. Provided *you* are making the choice (rather than your boss or clients), the freedom to do tasks and activities at a time that suits you best can really help to take some pressure off. It can also help you think more creatively about where you can get help, allowing you more freedom to choose how you use your time.

There are an increasing number of freelance people available to help support you where it counts – in the home you can get help with cleaning, child care, gardening and decorating. Do your shopping on the internet and get groceries, clothes and gifts delivered. Delegate cooking one night with a ready meal or takeaway. And if you're self-employed or running your own business, accountants, book-keepers, virtual assistants, copywriters, IT support and tax consultants can take some of the chores out of your day.

Obviously hiring help will cost money. But if you are already out of time and energy, what other resource is available to you to ease the stress and pressure? And paying for help in one sphere of life can help to ease pressure in another.

Automate

You might also find that you can use newer technologies to streamline your work. Clear some thinking space in your diary by letting your voicemail take your calls. Rather than allowing your day to be punctuated by the phone, you can condense telephone time into those periods you choose to call back. Use 'call-divert' to send calls to a colleague and trade slots where you provide cover for each other.

You can also hold meetings by phone rather than in person. Use teleconferencing or three-way calling when there are more than two of you – I guarantee your meetings will contain less waffle and be over more quickly.

Use the filters in your email software to pre-sort, prioritize and auto-respond to incoming messages. If you are on a lot of circulation lists, for example, you could set up the filters to divert these emails to a 'reading' folder so that they don't crowd out those messages that require a reply.

Eliminate

If all else fails and you still haven't enough time to get everything done, you may have to face up to readjusting your expectation of what is achievable. Perhaps it is time for certain tasks and activities to be dropped from your workload?

Check that you can identify your work goals. Then you can assess the extent to which each task on your things-to-do list will help you achieve them. When the answer is not clear, you may have found a candidate for elimination.

Things-to-do lists often contain what I call 'sediment' – those tasks that have sunk to the bottom of the list and have lain there a while. Why don't you just forget about them? If they are really that important, you don't need them on a list to remind you.

If you're feeling slightly anarchic, there's a strategy called *wait twice to be asked*. Running counter to the instructions of mothers everywhere, this is a way of testing whether the tasks that other people want you to do are really necessary. In one of my previous jobs, the marketing department used to come out of meetings full of great ideas. They'd fire off memos to us all asking for information, reports and advice. I discovered that if I waited twice to be asked, many of these tasks would drop off the agenda. It was only if they followed up with a reminder that I knew they really needed my input.

While this is a strategy that requires some care and judgment in its execution, waiting twice to be asked recognizes that the people around us also don't have time to do everything they'd like. Which I find reassuring.

■ I lack confidence/can't say 'no'

I have linked the issues of self-confidence with the ability to say 'no' because, while they sometimes have different causes, they are often both rooted in issues of assertiveness.

Gael Lindenfield's book, *Assert Yourself,* is a good place to start on exploring this topic further. Getting support from a coach can also help you work through your own specific issues related to this common obstacle to fulfilling your potential.

My own observation of clients who struggle with issues around confidence and assertiveness is that there is often a lack of clarity about rights and responsibilities. In particular, when you are put in a position of wanting to say no to a job that someone is asking of you, you may hold back because you are not clear whether the request is legitimate or not – or what the implications of saying no might be. While people have a perfect right to make requests of you, you are not obliged to please everybody. The interaction between people in the workplace is a continually shifting process of balancing needs. You can't fulfil your own potential if you are too busy helping others to satisfy theirs and saying 'yes' all of the time is a fast route to undermining your own confidence.

Assertiveness, amongst other things, requires you to be clear about your rights and needs and to learn key workplace skills of communication, negotiation and self-confidence. If this an issue that affects you, then it probably won't be resolved by changing your job but principally by changing yourself.

■ 'Rising above the stench'

This was a phrase coined by a client of mine to describe her own attempts to see past some of the obstacles in her workplace and focus on the underlying fulfilment that her work provides.

Danita is a development manager for a large charity that works in international development. The size of her organization means that there is a cumbersome hierarchy, with all the internal politics, opportunities for miscommunication and lack of coordination that this sometimes entails. Danita's work requires her to gain the cooperation of colleagues across the charity's different divisions and she is frequently frustrated by people's inability to make decisions, deliver projects on time or admit to their mistakes. The senior management team adds to the problem by changing its mind about strategic decisions and failing to allocate adequate resources to enable Danita and her team to fulfil their objectives.

Not surprisingly, she experiences periods of demotivation as well as high levels of stress, particularly when deadlines are looming and colleagues have not delivered on their commitments. As a result she often works long hours and takes work home with her at the weekend.

But Danita fundamentally supports the work of her organization and knows it makes a big difference to the lives of people in developing countries. She feels her role at the charity makes good use of her skills and abilities and, in spite of the frustrations some of them cause, she enjoys a good working relationship with many of her colleagues. In searching for meaning and fulfilment in her work, Danita does not feel she needs to seek a new job but rather to see past the frustrations in the workplace and focus on the positives – hence she will 'rise above the stench'.

Not surprisingly this is easier said than done. If you encounter daily frustrations and obstacles in your work, it is more than most people can do to ignore them and cheerfully whistle their troubles away. I'm always amazed by how much aggravation people will tolerate in the workplace. Most working people I encounter are dedicated to their jobs and committed to making the best of the situation. Things have to get *really* bad before they are prepared to walk away.

If you believe that you are in the right job for you but have some frustrations that prevent you from seeing that, then I hope some of the following approaches will help you in your quest to rise above the stench.

■ Maintain your integrity

If you've done the exercise on values earlier in the book, you will have a clear idea of what you need to maintain your integrity. If you feel pressured to behave in a way that is incongruous with your values, or find that your ways of coping with the job are tempting you to compromise on them, it is clearly time for a rethink. Being clear about your values means that you are able to draw a line which you won't cross and that can be helpful in making decisions about when to take action in resolving workplace dilemmas – or even decide when it is time to move on.

It never feels good to be put in a position where your integrity is undermined; any sense of fulfilment you have will quickly ebb away. You'll soon feel mired in the issues that block your performance and potential, rather than staying focused on aspects of your work that are meaningful to you. Use the work you have been doing as you've read through this book to help you stay the course in pursuing a fulfilling working life. Be prepared to take action if the nature of your work shifts you away from it.

■ Allow time for reflection

It is difficult to keep everything in perspective when you are up close to the everyday issues in your workload. Finding time and space to step back from the immediate tasks in hand to see the bigger picture can be a vital component of finding the meaning in your work. Everyone has their own preferred way for doing this, whether it is some kind of structured meditation or prayer, simply sitting quietly for a time or going for a walk, run or cycle ride.

Creating this kind of space for yourself regularly allows your mind to disengage from the immediate issues that preoccupy you and gain a better overview of your working life as a whole. It's an opportunity for your subconscious to reprioritize the issues you face and can help you generate new ideas or come up with solutions to problems.

I've had some of my best ideas on long train journeys. Simply sitting in a quiet carriage and watching the countryside roll by puts my brain in neutral which in turn allows it to roam freely over the landscape of my working life. Sometimes whole new creative ideas have come to me on the train, at other times I've simply realized that I needed to give attention to a neglected area of work. While you can't jump on an intercity train every time your work needs some perspective, there is always something you can do to help you detach from the proximity of your work and step back for a while. Some people find sitting silently for a short period of time each day helps them to regain perspective, while others keep a journal or do free association writing first thing in the morning. Time management expert Mark Forster suggests writing a list of 'what was better about today' each evening to take your mind away from what is still to be achieved, focusing instead on accomplishments and enjoyable moments. And countless people testify to the benefits of exercise not just on their body but on their mind as well.

Even when you are in a job you love, it is beneficial to find activities that complement the kinds of tasks that occupy your working hours. If you work alone, make a point of finding time with other people. If your job involves sitting at a desk, find something physical to do to offset it. Where your job doesn't require you to physically craft anything with your hands, find time to cook, garden, build or paint. Move from indoors to outdoors, 'head' to 'hands', crowd to solitude. These kinds of complementary activities will help put your mind and body back into balance, reconnecting you with your wider abilities, potential and creativity. Above all, they will take you away from the kind of environment that might be doing your head in and help you see that there is more to life than the workplace frustrations you are encountering.

In today's culture of overwork, with busy people trying to juggle home and work priorities, it is too easy to overlook recuperative time for yourself. Find something that works for you that can be realistically fitted into your daily routine – just twenty minutes of quiet time away from the buzz of the workplace and home can pay real dividends in helping you to rise above the stench.

■ Spend time with positive people

To put this another way, give moaners a wide berth. There's no hope of you holding on to any sense of the motivational rewards at work if you are surrounded by colleagues who constantly complain about what's wrong with the company or employer.

I know a lot of school teachers, for example, whose survival strategy is to avoid the staff room at all costs. If there is a culture of complaining in the school, how does it help to spend all one's break time listening to colleagues witter on about pupils' bad behaviour, the latest directive from the education authority or what a muppet the Head is? That's not a break: it's purgatory. For teachers who feel passionate about the rewards and impact of their work, it is very hard to stay in tune with its meaning if there is a constant soundtrack of misery every day.

Every workplace has its prophets of doom and – even if you sympathize with some of their views – they are best avoided. Spend time with colleagues who are excited by their work, focused on positive objectives and provide good role models for keeping the negative stuff in check.

■ Find a coach or mentor

You might also consider finding someone who can help you to make the most of the work you are in. A coach or mentor will help you take time to reflect on the positive aspects of your work and the way it connects to your vocational goals. They can help you think through your priorities and overcome obstacles to good performance.

A coach isn't there to give you advice or tell you what to do, although they might share insights or strategies that have worked for others in a similar situation to your own. A coach acts as a facilitator to help you step back from your work and take stock of where you are. They will encourage you to stay focused on your goals and help you plan a course of action for achieving them. Above all, they will listen to you as you try to make sense of complex issues or situations and help you pinpoint the action you can take to keep your work meaningful and fulfilling.

The word *mentor* in this context often means someone who is experienced in the same industry or profession as you and is able to bring their experience and insight of the industry into their coaching of you. They could be someone in the same company as you but outside your chain of command (which is important if you are going to be able to speak freely to them). Or they might have done the same job as you elsewhere – a management mentor, for example, may have been in management in an altogether different industry but nonetheless understands the issues and pressures faced by managers.

A *coach* may not have the same professional experience as you but will have been trained to support you in the same way as a mentor and may be a better choice if the issues you face are not specifically related to your profession. Many coaches have particular specialisms, such as helping clients plan a career change, start a business or improve time management. There are a plenty of web-based directories to help you locate a coach with the right experience or specialism to support you. It is important to find a coach with whom you have the right rapport, who understands the issues you face and with whom you feel able to be open. Many offer a free introductory consultation and it is well worth taking advantage of this to help you shop around for the right person.

Spending time with a coach or mentor can help to put your career back on track and drive you forward in making the changes to gain the level of meaning and purpose you seek in your work. As well as putting you in control of your career again, coaching often has a big impact on your self-confidence, motivation and ability to cope with the pressures of today's culture of work. Above all, a coach will help you to realize your potential and bring out the best you have to offer in creating a rewarding and meaningful working life.

■ To think about...

1. What aspects of work do you tend to avoid? What are the reasons for the avoidance, and what actions can you put in place to overcome them?
2. Are there issues with your colleagues, clients or boss that you need to resolve in order to restore your fulfilment at work? Which of the strategies above are appropriate to your situation?
3. What could you do to take time out and reflect on your working life? What are you already doing in this respect that you could expand to help you keep workplace frustrations in perspective and stay focused on fulfilling your potential?

Appendix

If any of the issues covered in this book have struck a chord with you and you would like support in taking action on them, or if reading this book raises any questions for you, you can email me at reader-enquiries@myworkinglife.com.

■ Further reading

Arnold, Johann Christoph, *The Lost Art of Forgiving*, Plough, 1998

Bridges, William, *Jobshift: How to Prosper in a Workplace Without Jobs*, Nicholas Brealey, 1995

Bronson, Po, *What Should I Do with My Life?*, Secker & Warburg, 2003

Bunting, Madeleine, *Willing Slaves: How the Overwork Culture is Ruling Our Lives*, HarperCollins, 2004

Cameron, Julia, *The Artist's Way: a Course in Discovering & Recovering Your Creative Self*, Pan, 1995

Covey, Stephen R., *The Seven Habits of Highly Effective People*, Simon & Schuster, 1994

Forster, Mark, *Get Everything Done and Still Have Time to Play*, Hodder & Stoughton, 2000

Ghazi, Polly and Jones, Judy, *Downshifting: The Guide To Happier, Simpler Living*, Coronet, 2004

Handy, Charles, *The Age of Unreason*, Arrow, 2002

Handy, Charles and Handy, Elizabeth, *Reinvented Lives: Women at Sixty – A Celebration*, Hutchinson, 2002

Lewin, Roger and Regine, Birute, *Weaving Complexity & Business: Engaging The Soul at Work*, Texere, 2001

Lindenfield, Gael, *Assert Yourself: Simple Steps to Getting What You Want*, HarperCollins, 2001

Nash, Susan, *Be a Successful Consultant: an Insider Guide to Setting Up and Running a Consultancy Practice*, How To Books, 2003

Pyke, Gary and Neath, Stuart, *Be Your Own Career Consultant: How to Unlock Your Career Potential*, momentum, 2002

Reeves, Richard, *Happy Mondays: Putting the Pleasure Back into Work*, momentum, 2001

Semler, Ricardo, *Maverick!*, Arrow, 2001

■ Useful websites

www.myworkinglife.com   *Fraser Dyer's website, detailing coaching services and free subscription to his e-newsletter*

www.9types.com   *online test for the Enneagram personality profile*

www.humanmetrics.com   *online Jung Typology Test*

www.peterhoney.co.uk   *online Learning Styles questionnaire*

www.profiler.com   *Campbell Interests and Skills Survey*

www.businesslink.org   *Government agency providing advice and support for small businesses and business start-ups*

www.do-it.org.uk   *National database of volunteering opportunities*

www.volunteeringengland.org.uk   *find your local Volunteer Centre in England*

www.volunteerscotland.info   *find your local Volunteer Centre in Scotland*

www.volunteering-ni.org   *find your local Volunteer Bureau in Northern Ireland*

www.volunteering-wales.net   *find your local Volunteer Bureau in Wales*

All Lion Books are available from your local bookshop,
or can be ordered via our website or from Marston Book
Services. For a free catalogue, showing the complete list
of titles available, please contact:

Customer Services
Marston Book Services
PO Box 269
Abingdon
Oxon
OX14 4YN

Tel: 01235 465500
Fax: 01235 465555

Our website can be found at:
www.lionhudson.com